Hallelujah
FOR THE
Day

Hallelujah FOR THE Day

An African Prayer Book

Edited by Anthony J. Gittins, CSSp

With a Foreword by Maurice J. Nutt, C.Ss.R.

Liguori/Triumph
LIGUORI, MISSOURI

Published by Liguori/Triumph
An imprint of Liguori Publications
Liguori, Missouri
www.liguori.org
www.catholicbooksonline.com

Some of this material was originally published in 1985 as *Heart of Prayer: African, Jewish, and Biblical Prayers* by Collins Liturgical Publications.

Scripture quotations are taken from the *New Revised Standard Version Bible*, copyright 1989, by the Division of Christian Education of the National Council of the Churches of Christ in the U.S.A. Used by permission.

Library of Congress Cataloging-in-Publication Data

Gittins, Anthony J.
    Hallelujah for the day : an African prayer book / edited by Anthony J. Gittins ; with a foreword by Maurice J. Nutt.
        p.   cm.
    Includes bibliographical references and index.
    ISBN 0-7648-0790-0 (pbk.)
    1. Africa—Religious life and customs. 2. Christians—Africa—Prayer-books and devotions—English. 3. Prayers. I. Gittins, Anthony J., 1943– II. Heart of prayer.

BR1360 .H25 2002
242'.8'0096—dc21   2001038873

Printed in the United States of America
06 05 04 03 02   5 4 3 2 1
Revised edition 2002

From my beloved Africa
These prayers are taken with gratitude
To my beloved grandchildren—
Jevette, Robin, Tony, and Reggia—
They are offerred with love.

Contents

||||||||

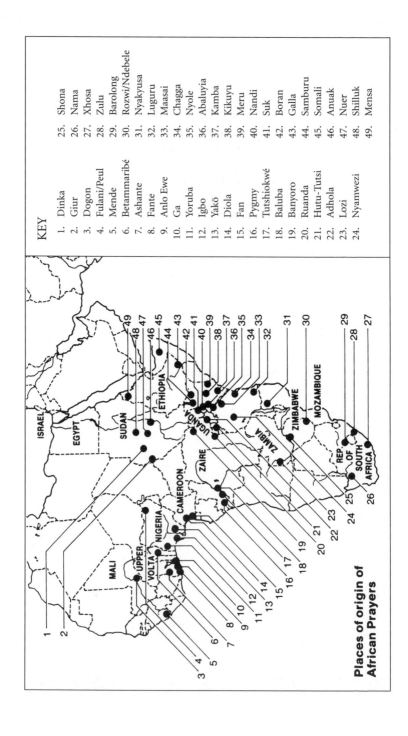

Places of origin of African Prayers

KEY

1. Dinka
2. Giur
3. Dogon
4. Fulani/Peul
5. Mende
6. Betammaribé
7. Ashante
8. Fante
9. Anlo Ewe
10. Ga
11. Yoruba
12. Igbo
13. Yakö
14. Diola
15. Fan
16. Pygmy
17. Tutshiokwé
18. Baluba
19. Banyoro
20. Ruanda
21. Hutu-Tutsi
22. Adhola
23. Lozi
24. Nyamwezi
25. Shona
26. Nama
27. Xhosa
28. Zulu
29. Barolong
30. Rozwi/Ndebele
31. Nyakyusa
32. Luguru
33. Maasai
34. Chagga
35. Nyole
36. Abaluyia
37. Kamba
38. Kikuyu
39. Meru
40. Nandi
41. Suk
42. Boran
43. Galla
44. Samburu
45. Somali
46. Anuak
47. Nuer
48. Shilluk
49. Mensa

Foreword

||||||||

*"The Christian prays in every situation, in his [or her]
walks for recreation, in his [or her] dealings with others,
in silence, in reading, in all rational pursuits."*

—SAINT CLEMENT OF ALEXANDRIA

■ Today many people are turning to the power of prayer to
help them cope with the situations and circumstances of life.
In these instances, they may or may not turn to their familiar,
memorized prayers of their youth. They often find themselves
seeking assistance from "well prayed prayers" found in books.
In fact, prayer books are becoming common-place and even
"bestsellers" in bookstores.

Hallelujah for the Day: An African Prayer Book is far from
being yet another prayer book. It distinguishes itself as unique
because it rediscovers the traditions of prayer from an African
perspective. The prayers contained in this anthology of prayers
may also be described as ancient and ascetic, earthy and East-
ern, sacred and soul-stirring, and lest we forget, pragmatic and
powerful. As an African American priest, these well-chosen
prayers, selected by Spiritan Father Anthony J. Gittins, afforded
me a *Sankofa* moment. The word *Sankofa* is Swahili which
means to "go back and fetch that which was lost." As a son of

the African diaspora, many of these prayers called me back to a place and time that I have never been and yet feel that I belong. These African prayers welcomed me "home" to "fetch a spiritual experience" that invited me to talk to the God of my ancestors—the God of ages past and Hope for years to come.

There has been some debate between African-American scholars of religion as to whether African-Americans have been able to retain much of their African religious heritage. It is believed by some scholars that with the breaking up or destruction of the clan and kinship organization, the religious myths and cults lost their significance. However, I contend that many contemporary religious expressions such as singing, praying, shouting, witnessing, testifying, "calling down the ancestors" and "telling the story," have all been retained from a rich African past. Though not purely African, the prayers and devotion of those of the African diaspora are expressed with African hearts and an African sacred memory.

While this is unquestionably a book of African prayers, it is not exclusively a book for Africans and their descendants. Africans are a communal people. Their spirituality and spirit is one of welcome and inclusiveness. I am sure that all readers, irregardless to one's race or nationality, will experience a *Sankofa* moment like I did. It is my hope and prayer for you that while meditating on these simple and yet profound prayers "Mother Africa" will call you "home."

You will discover that you have unearthed, yes, "fetched" something that you never knew you lost. Welcome home.

MAURICE J. NUTT, C.SS.R., D.MIN.
PASTOR, ST. ALPHONSUS LIGUORI "ROCK" CATHOLIC CHURCH
ST. LOUIS, MISSOURI

Introduction

||||||||

■ For those who like prayer books with formal prayers, we live in happy times; there are dozens of such books available. Ours is an age in which people are learning about, and experimenting with, many forms of prayer and methods of praying. Some people are helped by prayers in the form of prose or poetry, prayers with strong imagery or appeal to the senses or the social conscience; others prefer to pray straight from the heart, either with no books to assist them, or with a minimal use of written prayers, and then only to stimulate them to personal reflection, meditation, and union with God. Inasmuch as prayer is both communication and receptivity, any form of prayer which helps people in their quest for God is surely legitimate and valid.

In recent years, too, there has been an exciting rediscovery of traditions of prayer from the East and from world religions not previously very familiar to, or understood by, the majority of Christians.

Prayer is communion with God, whether in silence, song, or shouting, whether alone or in a group. Prayer books are no more than a means to that end. Some people may feel that they are not really praying unless they have a prayer book; others may find that they never have had a use for one. But a prayer book may be required or useful if a person finds difficulty in becoming centered in God. I find that to be the case, though not all prayer books, by any means, appeal to my taste; nevertheless, I do have quite a few and I certainly like to pray. I also find it helpful to know something about how other people pray, and what forms of prayer they find useful. And this brings me to the present collection.

Most of the prayers here assembled are somewhat different from the usual, and are offered to anyone who believes in God, anyone who wants to pray and would like some new ideas, and anyone who already prays. They are, more specifically, for those who accept Jesus Christ as Savior, and yet, with some exceptions, they do not mention the name Jesus and do not refer to him. This is quite deliberate. Any prayers which have ever been said to or about Jesus are either available to us now or are forever lost. But for Christians who want to think of God—Creator, Parent, Protector, Healer, and the like—as understood before or independently of the Incarnation, there are many prayers in existence whose riches are virtually unknown to praying believers.

Each society has its own repository of cultural riches, and there are many cultures in which such riches are in danger of being lost or devalued as they become assimilated into the literate and computerized cultures of the modern Western scientific world. Oral traditions can survive without being written down, but only if they are transmitted verbally. If the tradition is not maintained by word of mouth, it becomes forever lost. Writing helps to preserve traditions, not only among those who would otherwise forget them, but for the benefit of a wider audience. So, in the Bible, we have a written record of the Word of God which would otherwise have been irretrievably lost. Africa, a continent of almost unimaginable human and cultural riches, was, until recently, and much like ancient Israel, a land of oral rather than written traditions. Literacy helped destroy traditional African cultures, yet not all was lost. Many prayers and prayer-forms have been preserved, largely in academic or unpublished works, and are generally not available to the general reader.

This prayer book (it is not just a book of prayers but a book for praying) is offered, then, to all, but it has been compiled with two particular types of users in mind.

In the first place, it is for African-Americans who are unaware of, or unable to discover, their own cultural heritage of prayer. The African prayers included here contain, I believe, not only an intrinsic beauty, but a characteristically African style and urgency which is as redolent and evocative of authentic African worship. Whether Christian or not, African-Americans have a right to claim what is their own, and also have every justification for taking great pride in the aspirations and formulations of their forebears. I hope that this collection will appeal to African-Americans as an authentic expression of indigenous worship, and, as well, be an inspiration for further reflection and meditation.

Second, these prayers are offered directly, and with no apology, to people who are not African, wherever they may be. Just as any culture which is unaware of its antecedents is, to some extent, impoverished; in the same manner, any culture which cannot dip into the repository of other cultures is deprived of other perspectives and insights. Those who are not themselves African should not remain isolated from, or inured to, the living tradition of prayer which, while largely unfamiliar, is also refreshing and powerful.

Today, perhaps more than ever, believers must seek the unity for which Christ prayed. One way of doing this is to pool resources and allow oneself to become enriched from the vast stores of one another's wisdom. Africans, African-Americans, and others, including expatriates living in Africa, should be able to discover, in these prayers, some universally relevant aspirations and invocations.

A NOTE ON THE SOURCES

The tribal African prayers—some one hundred fifty from fifty African societies—have, obviously, been translated from other languages. In most cases, they appear as they are in the sources, if the sources are in English. Where the sources are in French, I have adopted a rather free form of translation. And even when I have taken prayers which were in English when I found them, I have, on occasion, changed certain words, paraphrased or presented the prayers in an adapted form. The reason is quite simple: this is not an academic or antiquarian book, but a praying book, and I have tried to maintain simplicity and freshness rather than a slavish adherence to first-published translations. (The sources from which these prayers are taken are listed in the Bibliography.)

All the prayers in this book must be understood as a reflection of their own appropriate backgrounds; they are "traditional" prayers which speak powerfully about the earth, crops, sickness, the powers of nature, fertility, death, and other fundamental issues in worlds that exist without nuclear bombs, genetic engineering, or widespread scientific advances. These are peasant or fishing communities and their prayers are fresh, urgent, and "earthy," though directed beyond the physical earth, but they show a love for and respect of this earth. They may serve to remind present-day non-Africans of a dimension of prayer which might otherwise be overlooked. They have a directness and an ingenuousness, a total lack of coyness and florid style, which contrasts beautifully with the many richly decorated and sometimes sentimental prayers so familiar to urbanized Christians. These prayers never appear sentimental and are often surprisingly frank. I hope they may bring all readers closer to a God who is neither remote in High Heaven nor merely a Westernized God, but a God of all nations, in the forests, or on the savannahs, as much as in the factories or in the cities.

If the imagery of some of the prayers is rather strange to our eyes: "God, the piler-up of the great rocks"; "let not our arrows miss the animals in the bush"; "if anyone should cast a spell over us, let him die," then we might remember that a great deal of Western Christian imagery is extremely alien to African minds. With empathy, information, and effort, things that appear to be strange and alien at first sight can become illuminating and precious. A God that is depicted as being "robed in splendor and coming in might," or sitting on a throne judging the nations, is as much a projection of those who try to attach labels to God as it is incomplete and, therefore, distorted as it stands. Perhaps these prayers will give pause for thought and open our eyes to the tender mercies of our God too: a God who, in the words of so many Samburu prayers, so touchingly, can respond to the requests of beloved children by saying, simply: "All right."

To the African, some of the unfamiliar prayers in this book may help promote a God who really does offer to human beings a developing relationship: a notion both novel to and difficult to understand for traditional Africa. And, for the person who is unfamiliar with African prayer, the Christian doctrine of the communion of saints may, perhaps, become more understandable through these African prayers which speak so eloquently of the essential unity of humankind and the crucial importance of group solidarity and community cooperation among all people, whether alive or dead. African prayers are closely rooted in the plight and the needs of the community, even when they ask for favors for an individual; we can all learn a lesson here.

As comparison and contrast, Chapter 18 presents prayers in a more familiar format and in more familiar words. Collected here are prayers of Africans such as Saint Augustine, Josephine Bakhita, Fulgentius of Ruspe, and Peter Martyr of Alexandria. This chapter gives only a brief indication of how the early Church flourished on the continent of Africa, especially in regions around the Mediterranean.

A NOTE ON THE LANGUAGE

Many images of God are presented in these pages; I hope they will give pause for thought. But many prayers in a more familiar style may sometimes obtrude, because they uncritically reflect a male orientation in the godhead. Such prayer-forms can be offensive, and so, wherever possible, and without destroying the imagery or flow of the prayers, I have tried to avoid sexist language, and worked to present a universal God who loves all people (not solely a God who made "man" and loves "him": not a God who cares for "his" people: not a God limited by our inappropriate language and labels).

If the male-oriented image of God is an intrinsic part of the prayer, I have, at times, left it unchanged. Those who pray these pages can, of course, feel free to modify the language as they see fit.

A NOTE ON THE STRUCTURE OF THE BOOK

Finally, a few remarks on the structure, presentation, and possible uses of this book. There are eighteen sections, each representing a stage or life-crisis, with which everyone should be able to identify. All the prayers in any given section carry the theme of that section, but may also have been included in a different section, the choice of the placement of each is our subjective means to present them to you in as user-friendly a way as possible. Of note, as well, is the inclusion of a "First Line Index" in which, as the title indicates, the first lines of each prayer are listed alphabetically, with their appropriate page references. This will help you find the full text of a prayer for which you remember only the first line.

Some of the prayers are presented in a straightforward prose fashion. Partly for cosmetic reasons, we present prayers in sections or stanzas, so that two or more persons or groups may share the prayers when reading aloud. Perhaps two sides of a church or a classroom may want to alternate, or simply two readers may provide variation in voice. A further reason for presenting many prayers in sections or stanzas is so that an individual, praying privately and silently by way of meditation, may take a small section for reflection, before passing on to another image or topic. There is absolutely no need to be limited to reading these prayers straight through; they are for praying, and prayer may take many different forms. I hope that the presentation will assist anyone—man, woman, American, African, European, catechist, lay leader, priest, student, prayer group, class, or congregation—discover and enjoy walking with God in prayer.

Finally, you will find the sources and acknowledgments at the book's end.

The Earth: God's Creation

||||||||

▶ God, Provider of Life

Creator God, we announce your goodness because it is clearly visible in the heavens where there is the light of the sun, the heat of the sun, and the light of night. There are rain clouds. The land itself shows your goodness, because it can be seen in the trees and their shade. It is clearly seen in water and grass, in the milking cows, and in the cows that give us meat. Your love is visible all the time: morning and daytime, evening and night. Your love is great. It has filled the land; it has filled people. We say: "Thank you, our God," because you have given us everything we have. You have given us our fathers and mothers, our brothers and sisters, our children and friends. You have given us cows, grass, and water. We have nothing except what you have given us. You are our shield; you protect us. You are our guard; you take care of us. You are our safety, all days. You stay with us for ever and ever. You are our father and mother. Therefore we say: "Thank you." We worship you with our mouths. We worship you with our bodies. We worship you with everything we have, because only you have given us everything. We say: "Thank you," today. And tomorrow. And all days. We do not tire in giving thanks to you.

MAASAI, KENYA AND TANZANIA

▶ We Drink In the Beauty of Your Creation

O Lord, O God,
creator of our land, our earth, the trees,
the animals and humans, all is for your honor.
The drums beat it out, and people sing about it,
and they dance with noisy joy that you are the Lord.

You also have pulled the other continents
out of the sea.
What a wonderful world you have made out of wet mud,
and what beautiful men and women!
We thank you for all the beauty of this earth.

The grace of your creation is like a cool day
between rainy seasons.
We drink in your creation with our eyes.
We listen to the birds' jubilee with our ears.
How strong and good and sure your earth smells,
and everything that grows there.

The sky above us is like a warm, soft Kente cloth,
because you are behind it,
else it would be cold and rough and uncomfortable.
We drink in your creation and cannot get enough of it.
But in doing this we forget the evil we have done.

Lord, we call you, we beg you:
tear us away from our sins and our death.
This wonderful world fades away.
And one day our eyes snap shut,
and all is over and dead
that is not from you.

We are still slaves of the demons
and the fetishes of this earth,
when we are not saved by you.

Bless us.
Bless our land and people.
Bless our forests with mahogany.
Bless our fields with cassava and peanuts.
Bless the waters that flow through our land.
Fill them with fish
and drive great schools of fish to our seacoast,
so that the fishermen in their unsteady boats
do not need to go out too far.
Be with the youth in our countries,
and in all Africa, and in the whole world.
Prepare us for the service that we should render.

ASHANTE, GHANA

▶ God, Our Great Elder

O my Father, Great Elder,
I have no words to thank you,
but with your deep wisdom
I am sure that you can see
how I value your glorious gifts.
O my Father, when I look upon your greatness,
I am overcome with awe.
O Great Elder,
ruler of all things on earth and in heaven,
I am your warrior, ready to act according to your will.

KIKUYU, KENYA

▶ God, Our Great Spirit

Great Spirit!
Piler-up of the rocks into towering mountains!
When you stamp on the stones
the dust rises and fills the land;
Hardness of the cliff;
Waters of the pool that turn
into misty rain when stirred.
Gourd overflowing with oil!
Creator who sews the heavens together like cloth,
knit together everything here on the earth below.
You are the one who calls the branching trees into life:
you make new seeds grow out of the ground
so that they stand straight and strong.
You have filled the land with people.

Wonderful one, you live
among the sheltering rocks.
You give rain to us people.
We pray to you, hear us,
O Strong One!
When we beg you, show your mercy.
You are in the highest places
with the spirits of the great ones.
You raise the grass-covered hills,
above the earth,
and you make the rivers,
Gracious one!

ROZWI, SOUTH AFRICA

▶ You Loved Me Before Creation

My Lord, you loved me
before the mountains were strong.
From long ago you anointed me.
I am the beginning of your way.

I am your work of old,
before the large stretches of land were strong;
and the fountains of water
that had not yet spouted strongly.

And the fountains and rivers
before they had flowed strongly
Jehovah created me before his way.

The depth was not yet there
I was already born,
he had not yet created this heaven
And also this earth.

The sun had not shone yet
in the space of this heaven.
And the moon had not yet shone
In the space of this earth.

ZULU, SOUTH AFRICA

▶ God, Creator of All Life

This prayer was composed by a first-generation Christian. It is included here because of its distinctive African style, and for its evocation of Old Testament prayer forms.

Thou art the great God—the one who is in heaven.
It is thou, thou Shield of Truth,
it is thou, thou Tower of Truth,
it is thou, thou Bush of Truth,
it is thou, thou who sittest in the highest,
thou art the creator of life,
thou madest the regions above.
The creator who madest the heavens also,
the maker of the stars and the Pleiades—
the shooting stars declare it unto us.
The maker of the blind, of thine own will didst thou
    make them.
The trumpet speaks—for us it calls.
Thou art the Hunter who hunts for souls.
Thou art the Leader who goes before us.
Thou art the Great Mantle which covers us.
Thou art he whose hands are wounded;
thou art he whose feet are wounded;
thou art he whose blood is a trickling stream—and why?
Thou art he whose blood was spilled for us.
For this great price we call,
for thine own place we call.

    XHOSA, SOUTH AFRICA

▶ Give Us Your Blessing

Open the windows of heaven,
give us your blessing!
Open the windows of heaven,
give us your blessing!
Our Maker, Our God,
sweet Creator of us, the church membership.
Open the windows of heaven,
give us your blessing!

FANTE, GHANA

2

The History of Our Salvation

IIIIIIII

OUR WORLD IS WONDERFUL; GOD SAVES IT

Here are two acts of belief, or creeds. They do contain the name of Jesus, unlike many of the other prayers in this book, and they indicate how Jesus came into our world.

▶ Credo One

We believe in God, the omnipotence of love.
God is the creator of heaven and earth;
this whole universe, with all its mysteries;
this earth on which we live, and the stars to which we travel.
God knows us from eternity, God never forgets
that we are made of the dust of the earth
and that one day we shall return again to it as dust.

We believe in Jesus Christ,
the only beloved Son of God.
For love of all of us,
he has willed to share our history, our existence with us.
We believe that God also wanted to be our God
in a human way.

God has dwelt as man among us,
a light in the darkness.
But the darkness did not overcome him.
We nailed him to the cross.
And he died and was buried.
But he trusted in God's final word,
and is risen, once and for all;
he said that he would prepare a place for us,
in his Father's house, where he now dwells.

We believe in the Holy Spirit,
who is the Lord and gives life.
And for the prophets among us,
he is language, power, and fire.
We believe that together we are all on a journey,
pilgrims, called and gathered together,
to be God's holy people.
for we confess freedom from evil,
the task of bringing justice
and the courage to love.

We believe in eternal life, in love that is stronger than death
in a new heaven and a new earth.

SOURCE UNKNOWN

▶ Credo Two

We believe in the one High God, who out of love created the beautiful world and everything good in it. He created man and woman, and wanted them to be happy in the world. God loves the world and every nation and tribe on the earth. We have known this High God in the darkness, and now we know him in the light. God promised in the book of his word, the Bible, that he would save the world and all the nations and tribes.

We believe that God made good his promise by sending his Son, Jesus Christ, a man in the flesh, a Jew by tribe, born poor in a little village, who left his home and was always on safari doing good, curing people by the power of God, teaching about God and humankind, showing that the meaning of religion is love. He was rejected by his people, tortured, nailed hands and feet to a cross, and died. He lay buried in the grave, but the hyaenas did not touch him, and on the third day he rose from the grave. He ascended to the skies. He is the Lord.

We believe that all our sins are forgiven through him. All who have faith in him must be sorry for their sins, be baptized in the Holy Spirit of God, live the rules of love, and share the bread together in love, to announce the Good News to others until Jesus comes again. We are waiting for him. He is alive. He lives. This we believe. Amen.

MAASAI, TANZANIA

3

Morning Prayers

‖‖‖‖‖‖‖

▶ Accept the Morning Greeting

God, accept the morning greeting;
earth, accept the morning greeting;
ancestors, trees, stones, everything,
accept the morning greeting;
you who have placed the stone,
    accept the morning greeting;
you who have balanced the steps,
    accept the morning greeting;
you who slept on beds, accept the morning greeting;
women who bore long-necked calabashes,
accept the morning greeting;
our old men have poured out a libation: take and drink.
If you have drunk, give me a long old age;
make me a gift of children;
let me reach next year.

DOGON, MALI

▶ Lord, We Give Thanks for Everything

Lord, my joys mount as do the birds, heavenwards.
The night has taken wings and I rejoice in the light.
What a day, Lord! What a day!

Your sun has burned away the dew
from the grass and from our hearts.
What erupts from us,
what encircles us this morning, is thanksgiving.

Lord, we thank you for all and everything.
Lord, I thank you for what I am,
for my body tall and broad,
despite the meager meals at school,
and although father has no work.
This body grows and grows
even with malaria in my blood.

Lord, I also thank you
for this job, which I found during my holidays.
I make good money;
the money for school lies already in father's trunk.
You can let me advance far, but I know
I can never outdo your trees.

Lord, I am happy this morning.
Birds and angels sing and I am exultant.
The universe and our hearts are open to your grace.
I feel my body and give thanks.
The sun burns my skin and I thank you.
The breakers are rolling towards the seashore,
the sea foam splashes our house.
I give thanks.

Lord, I rejoice in your creation,
and that you are behind it, and before,
and next to it, and above—and within us.

Lord, your sun is balmy,
it caresses the grass and the cassava out of the clay,
tops it with flowers,
draws out the mahogany,
throws birds into the sky,
and out of us it drums
a song of praise for you.

GHANA

▶ To Walk Straight on the Path

O God, you have prepared in peace the path I must follow to-day. Help me to walk straight on that path. If I speak, remove lies from my lips. If I am hungry, take away from me all complaint. If I have plenty, destroy pride in me. May I go through the day calling on you, you O Lord, who knows no other Lord.

GALLA, ETHIOPIA

▶ For a Peaceful Life

Morning of my God, I have been faithful to you all my days. God, allow me to proceed through a peaceful life. Grant me, God, to continue living in peace as long as you will allow it, or even forever. Grant me a life that does not wear out.

SAMBURU, KENYA

▶ For Everlasting Life

My God, my God, grant me a life that never ends. My God, grant me what is desired and goes on forever. My God, grant me what is searched for and does not end, because always I am like a little sheep that gives milk, and also I give honey from my land. "Shelter-of-the-lambs," hold me tight. My progenitor, my God, grant me what is desired. Grant me the life of my children. Watch over me during the night and the day. Watch over mothers. Grant me what never ends. God, be watchful, watch over my little ones, both cattle and people; watch always.

SAMBURU, KENYA

▶ Guide My Steps in Peace

O God,
you gave me peace to pass the night;
give me peace as well to pass the day.
Wherever my way may lead,
which you in peace laid out for me,
O God, guide my steps.
In speech, take falsehood away from me,
in hunger, take murmuring from me,
in fullness, take complacency from me.
I pass the day invoking you,
O lordless Lord.

GALLA, ETHIOPIA

▶ Bless Me

O sun, as you rise in the East through God's leadership,
wash away all evils of which I have thought throughout
      the night.
Bless me, so that my enemies will not kill me and my family;
guide me through hard work.
O God, show [give] mercy to our children who are suffering;
bring riches today as the sun rises;
bring all fortunes to me today.

ABALUYIA, KENYA

▶ Dawn of My God

My God, dawn of my God that rises,
I have preceded you.
Dawn of my God, that comes up from the East
and then goes to fall into the West,
grant us a good life and a lucky one within our hearts.
In fact, we have come before you
so that, my God, you may grant us blessed hearts.
And God said: "All right."

SAMBURU, KENYA

▶ God, the Word

In the beginning was God,
today is God, tomorrow will be God.
Who can make an image of God? God has no body.
God is a word which comes out of your mouth.
That word! It is no more, it is past, and still it lives!
So is God.

PYGMY, ZAIRE

▶ Bless My Hand, My Creator

May the God of peace be with me;
may God help me;
may God give me peace.
In the name of God, my hand,
my creator, my hand.
May God give me the blessing of the weaver.
From the morning to the evening may I remain seated.
Who is the creator of the woven thread?
It is I. I am the creator of the weaver's thread.

PEUL/FULANI, WEST AFRICA

▶ God, Be Our Safeguard

May God agree with us.
Yes, my God, you will save us;
yes, my God, you will guide us,
and your thoughts will be with us night and day.
Grant us to remain a long time
like the great wing of rain, like the long rains.
Give us the fragrance of a purifying branch.
Be the support of our burdens,
and may they always be untied,
the shells of fertility and mothers and children.
God be our safeguard, also where the shepherds are.
God, sky, with stars at your sides
and the moon in the middle of your stomach,
morning of my God that is rising,
come and hit us with your blessed wind:
flood us with your waters.
And God said: "All right."

SAMBURU, KENYA

▶ To Be Safe

Morning has risen;
God, take away from us every pain,
every ill, every mishap;
let us come safely home.

PYGMY, ZAIRE

▶ God Glistens on the Grasses

Morning has risen;
Sleep is still in our eyes,
but at once on our lips
shall be your praise.
We glorify, praise and adore you.
We, that is, the earth,
the water, and the sky;
that is, the grasses and bushes and trees;
that is, the birds, and all the other animals;
that is, the people here on earth.
Everything that you have created
enjoys your sun and your grace.
Dawn glistens on the grasses.
Mist is still hanging in the trees.
And a soft wind promises a fine day.
Should we not enjoy everything
that you have created?
We are meant to.
That is why we are so joyful this dawn.
O, Lord, grant that the hours and minutes
do not slip away in our hands,
but that we may live in your time. Amen.

GHANA

▶ God, Protect Our Elders

May God protect our elders when they walk and when they stop, every day…in the morning that always rises…because, my God, we are always blind, my God, we are always ignorant and do not have eyes to see. My God, we pray you. My God, we pray you, grant us feet; grant us feet to walk with. Grant us to taste your fruits; grant me to taste your fruits. May it be so, my God. Thank you very much, my God.

SAMBURU, KENYA

▶ The Teacher's Prayer

Wonderful, merciful God,
I put myself in your hands with the first breath this morning.
I know you are alive,
I know your goodness and grace have no end.
I beg you, heavenly Father, take my day in your hands.
Push away all the temptations and wants of this day,
as you push away threatening storm clouds.
Let me do my work,
let me do it so that it is good for the boys and girls
and glorifies your name.
Give me right words and power and love,
so that your image may be rightly painted
for the children in the school.
Let your love and patience
be in everything I have to teach the children.
May my work be fruitful. Amen.

GHANA

4

Praise and Thanksgiving

||||||||

▶ For Food

Thank you very, very much;
my God, thank you.
Give me food today,
food for my sustenance every day.
Thank you very, very much.

SAMBURU, KENYA

▶ For Remedies

The year has come round, O great God,
never can we thank you for your deeds and blessings for us.
Come now and eat from our hands and bless your people.
Let all who are ill get well.
Let all who are barren bear children.
Let all who are impotent find remedy.
Do not let them go blind or paralyzed.
We beseech happiness, let us have it.

ASHANTE, GHANA

▶ Select Wisdom

Wisdom is the finest beauty of a person.
Money does not prevent you from becoming blind.
Money does not prevent you from becoming mad,
Money does not prevent you from becoming lame.
You may be ill in any part of your body,
so it is better for you to go and think again
and to select wisdom.
Come and sacrifice, that you may have rest in your body,
inside and outside.

AFRICAN

▶ Our King

Great is, O King,
our happiness in thy kingdom

We dance before thee, our king,
by the strength of thy kingdom.

May our feet be made strong;
let us dance before thee, eternally.

Give ye praise, to him above
who is worthy of praise.

ZULU, SOUTH AFRICA

▶ A Fisherman's Prayer

This is a prayer from a fisherman of Ghana; it is influenced by Christian ideas and language.

Lord, I sing your praise
the whole day through, until the night.
Dad's nets are filled; I have helped him.
We have drawn them in, stamping the rhythm with our feet,
the muscles tense.
We have sung your praise.

On the beach there were our mothers,
who bought the blessings out of the nets,
out of the nets and into their basins.
They rushed to the market, returned and bought again.
Lord, what a blessing is the sea, with fish in plenty.
Lord, that is the story of your grace:
nets tear, and we succumb because we cannot hold them.
Lord, with your praise we drop off to sleep.
Carry us through the night.
Make us fresh for the morning.
Hallelujah for the day!
And blessing for the night! Amen.

GHANA

5

Food, Crops, Planting, and Harvesting

|||||||||

▶ For Prosperity

Whoever is not prosperous,
may that one enjoy immeasurable prosperity.
Those who are fishermen among us,
if they go out with their nets
may their nets bring them prosperity.
If anyone should wish evil to follow the nets
may this evil come upon the one who plans this evil.
May we enjoy good health
so that we may all continue to serve you.
Women, men, and relations of every degree
may they all be safe and sound.
May we never suffer any evil.
May peace abound forever.
May it come to rain
so that our crops may produce abundantly,
and when we sell them
they must earn plenty of money to fill our rooms
so that we can continue to serve you.

ANLO EWE, GHANA

▶ Let Peace Reign

May our yams,
which we are going to plant in the earth this year,
be good.
May children be born.

May we have enough to eat.
Let us live.
If anyone should cast a spell over anyone else,
let that one die.
Let peace reign among us.

YAKÖ, NIGERIA

▶ To Make Good Use of the Power Granted Us

O God, you are the creator of all. Today we your creatures prostrate ourselves before you in supplication. We have no strength.
You who have created us have all power. We bring you our seed
and all our implements, that you may bless them and bless us
also, so that we may make good use of them by the power which
comes from you, our creator.

LOZI, ZAMBIA

▶ For Abundance and Health

The edges of the years have met,
I take sheep and new yams and give that you may eat.
Life to me. Life to this my Ashante people.
Women who cultivate the farms, when they do so,
grant that the food comes forth in abundance.
Do not allow any illnesses to come.

ASHANTE, GHANA

▶ For Fruitfulness

Yes! Yes! I implore you, O grandfathers who completed so many noble undertakings! Having sacrificed this bull which belongs to you, I pray to you, asking of you every kind of prosperity. I cannot deny you nourishment, since you have given me all the herds that are here, and if you ask of me the nourishment that you have given me, is it not just that I return it to you? Grant us many beasts to fill these tables! Grant us much grain, so that many people may come to inhabit this village which is yours and so may make much tumult to your glory. Grant us numerous offspring, so that this village may be much populated and your name may never be extinguished!

ZULU, SOUTH AFRICA

▶ Bless This

Creator Lord,
through whom everything on this earth grows—
sweet bananas, fat plantains, sour oranges,
dry yams, rice, corn, and peanuts
from which our good soups are squeezed—
who lets the sharp red peppers grow
that keep us healthy and burn stomachs clean;
who lets fresh water burst from the ground,
good, fresh water.
Bless this, my loving God and Father.
And see to it that all the atoms are in their right places.
    Amen.

GHANA

▶ For Safety From Evil

The time of harvest is over;
you have given us good crops;
we are going into the bush.
Now I call on you,
so that no evil falls on us
and our feet do not step on anything bad,
and that we meet nothing but good things
and that nothing bad touches us:
you guaranteed these things
and have kept your promise.
May the animals in the bush come to meet us;
let them come within our circle.
Let our arrows not miss them;
let our arrows kill them.
Let the arrows not kill any of us.
You who have given such a good harvest
continue to walk before us
as you have been doing for our grandparents.

BÉTAMMARIBÉ (SOMBA), DAHOMEY (BENIN)

▶ God, Take Your Portion

O God, you have formed heaven and earth;
you have given me all the goods that the earth bears!
Here is your part, my God. Take it!

PYGMY, ZAIRE

▶ Success for Our Crops

Hail, hail, hail.
May happiness come.
May meat come.
May corn come.
Just as the farmers work
and look forward to the reaping,
so may we sit again as we are sitting now.
May our enemies turn from us and go…
Lord, return.

GA, GHANA

▶ Feed Our Hungry Brothers and Sisters

O Lord, the meal is steaming before us
and it smells good!
The water is clear and fresh.
We are happy and satisfied.
But now we must think of our brothers and sisters
all over the world
who have nothing to eat
and only a little to drink.
Please, please give all of them your food and your drink.
That is the most important thing!
But also give them what they need every day,
to go through this life.
Now, and in all times,
give food and drink to our hungry brothers and sisters.
Amen.

GHANA

6

Faith, Trust, and Peace

‖‖‖‖‖‖

▶ So We No Longer Have Doubts

For your blessing we thank you, God: faith in you.
Increase it, we beg, so that we no longer doubt.
Drive out all our miserliness,
    so that we do not refuse you anything.
Increase our faith, for the sake of those without faith.
Make us instruments of your faith, for those with only
    a little.
Fill our bodies with faith, our bodies that work for you
    all our days.
Help us to avoid the enemies of our faith,
    or to overcome them.
You are with us in confrontations; this we believe.
In your hands we place ourselves, and are secure.
Make haste to enter our hearts; make haste.

MAASAI, TANZANIA

▶ For Danger to Pass By

Good God of this earth, my Lord,
you are above me, I am below.
When misfortune comes to me,
just as the trees keep off the sun from me
so may you take away misfortune.
My Lord, be my shadow.

Calling on you, I pass the day;
calling on you, I pass the night.
When the moon rises, do not forget me;
when I rise, I do not forget you.
Let the danger pass me by:
God, my Lord, you are the sun with thirty rays.

God, you hold the bad and the good in your hand;
my Lord, do not allow us to be killed,
we, your little ones, are praying to you.
A person who doesn't know the difference between good
and bad cannot make you angry;
once he does know and is unwilling to behave accordingly,
this is wicked—treat him as you think fit.

God, you made all the animals and people
that live upon the earth;
also, the corn on the earth where we live—
you made that too; we have not made it.
You have given us strength.
You have given us cattle and corn.

We worked the land and the seed grew up for us.
People were satisfied
with the corn which you allowed to grow for us.

The corn in the house has been burnt up;
who has burnt the corn in the house?
You know who it was.

You have allowed all this to be done;
why have you done this?
You know.
You show before our eyes
the corn which you allowed to grow.
The hungry look at it and are comforted.

When the corn blooms, you send butterflies
and locusts into it—locusts and doves.
All this comes from your hand.
Have you caused this to happen?
Why have you done this?
You know why.

If you love me
set me free, I beg you from my heart;
if I do not pray to you from my heart you do not hear me.
If I pray to you with my heart,
you know it and you are kind to me.

BORAN, KENYA

▶ May We Have No Accidents

May accidents stay far away from us. Leave freshness in the
village. Let everyone live. May everything be fresh and cool and
peaceful. May accidents stay far away. May the people do the
farmwork in peace. Let no fire burn us.

YAKÖ, NIGERIA

▶ Surround Your Children With Your Power, Lord

You, Father, who do not die,
you who do not know death
and whose life is always so animated
without knowing the cold sleep of death,
all your children have come here.

They have all gathered round you.
Surround them with your power, O Father.
May your shade penetrate into them,
you, Father, who do not die,
you, Father of our people.

FAN, CAMEROON-CONGO

▶ My Only Help in Misery

I have no other helper than you, no other father,
no other redeemer, no other support.
I pray to you. Only you can help me.
My present misery is too great.
Despair grips me, and I am at my wits' end.
I am sunk in the depths, and I cannot pull myself up or out.
If it is your will, help me out of this misery.
Let me know that you are stronger
than all misery and all enemies.
O Lord, if I come through this, please let the experience
contribute to my and my brothers' blessing.
You will not forsake me; this I know. Amen.

GHANA

▶ For Honesty in Business

Buyers and sellers,
God, you know, in our country these people are quite special,
but nobody can fool you, neither the buyer
nor those who sell.
It is not just a trifle over which we can make merry.
There can be fraud while people are hungry.
Others pile up their riches.
God, whether we buy or sell, let us stick to this.
We are quite willing to pay the value of the goods
but others should not overcharge.
God, make peace here as well. Amen.

GHANA

▶ O God, Lead My Steps

O God, you have let me pass the night in peace,
let me pass the day in peace.
Wherever I may go upon my way
which you made peaceable for me,
O God, lead my steps.
When I have spoken, keep lies away from me.
When I am hungry, keep me from murmuring.
When I am satisfied, keep me from pride.
Calling upon you, I pass the day,
O Lord who has no Lord.

BORAN, KENYA

▶ God Has Turned Away

God has turned his back on us;
the words of men have made him angry.
And yet he will turn round again.
God has turned his back on us.
We are the children of our Maker
and are not afraid that he will kill us.

DINKA, SUDAN

▶ Remove Us From Evil

Our Father, it is your universe,
it is your will, let us be at peace;
let the souls of your people be cool;
you are our Father, remove all evil from our path.

NUER, SUDAN

7

Trials and Disasters, Famine and Drought

‖‖‖‖‖‖

▶ I Am Hungry, Feed Me

God of our ancestors,
I lie down without food,
I lie down hungry,
although others have eaten and lie down full.
Even if it be but a polecat or a little rock-rabbit,
give me and I shall be grateful.
I cry to God. Ancestor of my ancestors.

BAROLONG, SOUTH AFRICA

▶ The Lord Gives Life

The source of being is above,
which gives life to all people;
For people are satisfied, and do not die of famine,
For the Lord gives them life,
that they may live prosperously
on the earth and not die of famine.

ZULU, SOUTH AFRICA

▶ God, Be Our Children's Guardian

My God, have mercy on our children
who were late in getting up.
My God, do not lead our children to ruin.
My God, our life is in our children.
My God, give us children, both small and big.
My God, be the guardian of our children
that are away in order to feed
our cattle in any grassland.
My God, I am old and near death
and my house needs help.
You be the guardian of all creatures.
Let it be so, my God.
Answer kindly to the words that we have said to you.
And God answered affirmatively.

SAMBURU, KENYA

▶ Give Us Rain

O Chief who has left me in this world at your death,
I come to offer the sacrifices.
Rain has ceased to fall in our country long ago.
Give us rain! Here is your water!
Give us rain! Let it rain!
Why do you leave me in trouble, you my Lord?
I have inherited your power. I did not usurp it.
You have left me in trouble.
If you continue and it does not rain in the land,
the inhabitants will go away.
Look, here is the goat, and here is your sheep!

NYAMWEZI TANZANIA

▶ For an End to Theft

Here is your cow, your food.
We pray to God. May theft go away.
Give us food and beans and millet,
      may we eat and be satisfied....
It is said that the sweet potatoes are scarce now, help us.
You, God, this is your cow,
God, this is your meat.
I shall seek another also which we shall give you like this.
May the locusts go away.
It is you who have caused theft because there is hunger.
At night, since we eat scraps of food our bellies
      are disquieted....
May we be satisfied.
People are eating millet porridge;
when food is plentiful they say it's horrible.
When someone eats millet porridge he dies,
      it kills a man.
We pray to him, this God, because we do not know him,
so we say: "You drive away the hunger.
Give all of us, God's people, food and hear us all."

   NYAKYUSA, TANZANIA

▶ Give Rain to Your People, Lord

You who give sustenance to your creatures, O God,
Put water for us in the nipples of rain!

You who poured water into oceans, O God,
Make this land of ours fertile again!

Accepter of penance, O God,
Gather water in rivers whose beds have run dry!

You who are glorious, truly bounteous, O God,
Our cries have undone us, grant a shower of rain!

You who are clement, truly worshiped, O God,
Milk water for beasts which are stricken with thirst!

Creator of nature who made all things, O God,
Transmute our ruin to blessing and good!

You who are merciful and compassionate, O God,
Milk rain from the sky for those in need!

Giver of victuals at all times, O God,
Who can do what you want, bestow on us rain!

Recorder of merit, who requites us, O God,
Into scorched empty ponds pour us water of rain!

You who are truthful, creator, O God,
We accept in submission whatever you say!

You who mete out good and evil, O God,
In this land we are broken, milk the clouds from above.

The darkness of night you transfigure, O God,
And make daylight follow; milk the sky lavishly!

You who gave brightness to sunshine, O God,
And know its principles, give us brown water from rain!

You who open all and give sustenance, O God,
People have scattered; send forth healthy rain!

Almighty, perfecter of counsels, O God,
Pour for us rain which would make the land wet!

You who are bounteous, the protector, O God,
We cannot survive drought, send us rain from your store!

You who drive the air which sways the trees, O God,
It is you whom we praised, grant us the goodness of rain!

You who are worshiped and answer prayers, O God,
Make the rain spread over the whole of the land!

Bestower of victories, benefactor, O God,
Bring us faultless rain which makes us dwell where it falls!

You who are one and are trusted, O God,
Provider of all, give water to your people!

SOMALI, SOMALIA

▶ For Rain

Heart return to the place. The seeker of the thing has found it.
Drawer, bring the little bud of the water of the rain. God send
us a great spreading rain, that the little boys may eat for themselves the herbs and salad plants of the deserted homesteads.

SOUTH AFRICA

▶ Avert This Evil

All our forebears, come and eat kola.
All those who gave us birth, come and hear.
Quell the quarrel,
quell the hot exchange of words.
We are not the first to err, neither the last.
This is your white hen and these are the yams.
The mistake has been made;
it will not happen again.
Avert this evil. Avert this evil. Avert this evil.
The invisible spirits that molest us,
eat this and be appeased.

IGBO, NIGERIA

8

Blessings

IIIIIIIII

▶ The Fire Blessing

When people are handed the fire at the end of the ceremony they are blessed with these words.

Receive this holy fire.
Make your lives like this fire.
A holy life that is seen.
A life of God that is seen.
A life that has no end.
A life that darkness does not overcome.
May this light of God in you grow.
Light a fire that is worthy of your heads.
Light a fire that is worthy of your children.
Light a fire that is worthy of your fathers.
Light a fire that is worthy of your mothers.
Light a fire that is worthy of God.
Now go in peace.
May the Almighty protect you
today and all days.

MAASAI, TANZANIA

▶ May God Be Good

May God raise you up
above everything.
Spread out like water of a lake.
Be abundance that never ends,
that never changes.
Be like a mountain.
Be like a camel.
Be like a cloud—
a cloud that brings rain always.
And God promised that it would be so.

SAMBURU, KENYA

▶ May God Bless You

May God go with you!
Go nicely: may your path be swept of danger.
God go with you, and may you escape
    from the mishaps ahead!
May you go with God!
Let God bear you in peace like a young shoot!
May you meet with the Kindly Disposed One!
May God take care of you!
May God walk you well!
May you pass the night with God!
May you remain with God!
May God be with you who remain behind!
May you stay with God!

VARIOUS AFRICAN BLESSINGS

▶ Father, Bless This Fire

Thank you Father for your free gift of fire.
Because it is through fire that you draw near to us
every day.
It is with fire that you constantly bless us.
Our Father, bless this fire today.
With your power enter into it.
Make this fire a worthy thing.
A thing that carries your blessing.
Let it become a reminder of your love.
A reminder of life without end.
Make the life of these people to be baptized like this fire.
A thing that shines for the sake of people.
A thing that shines for your sake.
Father, heed this sweet smelling smoke.
Make their life also sweet smelling.
A thing sweet smelling that rises to God.
A holy thing.
A thing fitting for you.

MAASAI, TANZANIA

▶ For Goodness to Remain

May we stay well in this country; we did not know that we
would arrive here. May we stay with peace and only have pleas-
ant dreams; the God of old, the Sun, when it rises in the East,
may it bring us honey, and when it goes to set in the West may
it take the badness with it.

NYOLE (ABALUYIA), KENYA

▶ For Prosperity, Health, Children, and Long Life

May the rising sun expose all wicked people.
East, I invoke your presence; West, I call upon you too.
O Heaven, your attention please.
I also invoke the presence of your beloved Earth.
God, the Almighty, the Great Creator,
who makes the hands and the feet,
I fervently invoke your presence.
Attention please…
I am only an ignorant child before you.
All Chiefs and Elders, peace be with you,
grant that all misfortunes return whither they
rightly belong.
May our world know only peace.
Grant good health to all your male servants.
Grant good health to all your female servants too.
Grant that our ears hear only the message of life,
and our eyes see only that which is life-giving.
Give us good health.
Do not allow us to be confined to the heat of the sick bed,
but grant that we bask forever outside in the rays
of the life-giving sun.
Whenever both your male and female servants engage in
any venture
please remove all difficulty from their way,
that they succeed abundantly.
Bless those who have no children with plenty of children,
and grant an increase to those who already have children.
Grant good health to the farmer,
that his hoe may find enough work to do
and the harvest far outweigh his labor.

When the fisherman goes out in his canoe,
grant that he direct his canoe to where the fish are,
that his net may have a good catch.
Grant that the catch may safely reach home.
Please drive away all kinds of inedible fish
and allow us to catch only the edible,
and very plentifully.
Help our traders, too, that they may succeed in all that they do.
Indeed, whatever your male and female servants do,
let your presence be with them always.
Let no one die prematurely.
It is for good health that we pray.
Grant that all manner of misfortunes may be far from us.
From his sons and daughters the buffalo drives away all
poverty as year succeeds year.
Worship should never consist of events to be counted.
Grant a constant good health to all…
To the masons and the carpenters, grant increased skill
in their work.
To the traders, grant success when they set out with their wares.
Good health to all.
Long life and prosperity to all.

ANLO EWE, GHANA

▶ For Plentiful Blessings

Bless this tree; make it grow; let it be entirely a blessing without any evil. Remove all evil; let it not come but let only the good come. Give your blessing that we may increase in all things and grow in plenty and be free from disease. Let blessings abound.

BANYORO, UGANDA

▶ For a Sweet and Everlasting Life

Spread out all your days.
May your children and cattle be plentiful
like down of lichens clinging to citron trees
    on the mountains.
Be fragrant like a fragrant resin.
May God grant you to last a long time.
May you have a fragrance of sweet life always, without end.

SAMBURU, KENYA

▶ May God Be With You

May God grant you a tranquil night.
May God support you during the day.
May God grant you shadow in the evening
and in the morning, all your days.

SAMBURU, KENYA

▶ To Always Rise Higher

My God, grant me a life that never ceases.
My God, may I always spread out.
My God, destroy hatreds that hate me.
My God, may I proceed with a life that endures
through generations, both living and not living.
Grant me, then, God, to always rise higher and higher.
And God said: "All right."

SAMBURU, KENYA

9

Women, Mothers, and Children

||||||||

▶ To Heal a Mother

God agrees: let us pray to God.
When I pray for this woman, God, agree with us.
God, do not be annoyed.
God, let her not die;
do not take her away from her children.
God, grant her to guide them.
God, agree to this.
God, grant that she may still remain
together with her children:
do not take her away from all of us, this mother.
God, who gives us rain, do not take this mother from us.
Give us back her spirit: give it back to us,
for us and for her children, and for her mother,
and for this group of elders, so many of them,
and for all who intercede for this woman.
God, agree with us.

SAMBURU, KENYA

▶ Litany

Leader: Thou, God, who art our Father and hast
created all of us,
thou knowest that this woman is ours,
and we wish her to bear children—

All: Grant children to her!

Leader: Should we die tomorrow, no children of ours
will remain—

All: Grant children to her!

Leader: If she bears a son,
his name will be the name of his grandfather.
If she bears a daughter,
her name will be the name of her grandmother.

All: Grant children to her!

Leader: Would it be displeasing to thee if many children
surrounded us?
Spirit of the father,
spirit of the grandfather,
you who dwell now in the skies,
are you displeased that we ask for children?

All: Grant children to her!

Leader: Should we die without them, who will guard
the family?
Your name and ours shall be forgotten
upon the earth.

All: Grant us this night good dreams,
that we will die leaving many children behind us.
GIUR, SUDAN

▶ Help My Sick Child

O God, you are great,
you are the One who created me,
I have no other.
God, you are in the heavens,
you are the only one:
now my child is sick,
and you will grant my desire.

ANUAK, SUDAN

▶ If You Only Would Help Me!

O God, if only you would help me!
O God of pity, God of my father's house,
if only you would help me!
O God of the country of the Hutu and Tutsi,
if only you would help me just this once!
O God, if only you would give me
a homestead and children!
I prostrate myself before you.
I cry to you: give me offspring,
give me as you give to others!
God, what shall I do, where shall I go?
I am in distress, where is there room for me?
O merciful, O God of mercy, help this once.

HUTU AND TUTSI, BURUNDI

▶ For Help During a Difficult Birth

You who are causing this difficult birth,
support our sister during her labor.
We bring you this chicken and this flour.
We beg you! Our lips are dry like dead leaves.
Help us, so that she may safely deliver her child.
The proverb says: where there are men there are axes,
wherever there are men they split and multiply.
Those who are born and those who remain after us
will remain to pay you honor.
But if you act like this, will there be anyone left
to pay you honor?
Help us now, so that she delivers a healthy baby,
in such a way that her womb may be refreshed.
You, God on high, we beg you: have pity on us.
See how our lips are dried up in our mouths.
We are begging you, Lord, help us,
so that your man-child may be saved,
and so that our hearts may rest easy.
Have pity on this little child, and on every little child
who is giving increase to the world.
What good will be served if this present situation
results in death?
We are begging you, Lord God.

TUTSHIOKWÉ, CONGO

▶ Strengthen Me and My Children

God, Supreme Being, Lord,
may I and my children become extremely strong
like the ant and the blacksmith's hammer,
like the iron in the forge.
May the jealous man not stretch out his hand against us.
May the witch die by that death which he deals out
    to others.
You, water which gives salt to the earth,
sun which cannot be looked upon directly,
whoever tries will be struck down by lightning—
here is the offering of cooked manioc.
Make my child extremely strong.
Even if you have to go to the ends of the earth,
still everything belongs to you.
God, go before us; the whole earth is under your control.

    BALUBA, CONGO

▶ Look After Our Children

O God, we beseech you to deliver us;
look after us,
look after our children.

    YORUBA, NIGERIA

▶ For the Health of My Child

Today I bring you out of the birthing-room.
There has never been any sickness in my house;
there has never been any epidemic around my house;
there has never been any death in my house,
today I show you your child—he is also my own.
When you chop down a tree, you always try
     to make it topple.
If you hit it with an axe and don't make it fall,
it is not defeated.
May this child not be struck down by sickness in body,
or head or chest or stomach.
May he not be stricken by sickness.
You are the Lord and master of this child.
This child shows us the new way,
and his mother will bear more children.

BÉTAMMARIBÉ (SOMBA), DAHOMEY (BENIN)

Men

||||||||

▶ For Strength in My Life

God of the skies, Lord, give me strength in my life, so that I may be strong. Give me well-being. May I marry a wife and father children. May I raise goats and chickens. May I obtain money and all kinds of goods. May I continue to flourish with life and health. My daughters are daughters coming from God. My sons are also his children. All I have is his. He is master of it all.

God, Supreme Being; God, Master of the earth; you who have created everything, I am here before you and the reason why I have come here is to obtain strength in my life.

May no wild beast come upon me;
may no thunderbolt or lightning strike me;
may no sorcerer see me;
and may no man with evil intentions look on me.

BALUBA, CONGO

▶ Bless Us and All We Have

We know you God, Chief, Preserver,
you who united the bush and the plain,
you, Lord, Chief, the Elephant indeed.
We praise you and pray to you and fall before you.
You have sent us this bull which is of your own fashioning.
Chief, receive the bull of your name.
Heal him to whom you gave it, and his children.
Sow the seed of offspring within us, that we may beget
    like bees.
May our clan hold together that it be not cleft in the land.
May strangers not come to possess our groves.
Now Chief, Preserver, bless all that is ours.

CHAGGA, TANZÁNIA

▶ God, Grant Me Children and Keep Me From Evil

My God, give me a belt in which there are sons and in which there are daughters. Grant me the intense yearning all people have concerning cattle and concerning the heart. God, agree with me.

Do not tell untruth; do not damage other people's things, because it is evil; because if you do, God abhors it.

When you are traveling and see someone else's things, be it also food that its owner had hidden, do not eat it. And if you do eat it, notify the owner, because, if you tell him, that is a good thing and God appreciates it. Instead, if you steal it, it generates hatred in the hearts of everybody, and God abhors it. God has agreed.

SAMBURU, KENYA

▶ Keep Me Safe From Sickness and Misfortune

God, be propitious to me!
Keep every sickness far from me,
Stop the wicked one who is contemplating my misfortune:
let any wicked plans fall on that person.
O God, be propitious to me!
Desert me not in my need:
give me children and wealth.
Lead to my house guests of happiness, O God!

DIOLA, CAMEROON

▶ For a Job

Here I am, sitting on the wall, waiting for a job.
I count the men, sitting nearby waiting for work.
Lord, can't you do something so that there is more work
and the bosses are more just?
And it hurts me that once again
I can take nothing home to my children and wife.
But I will not complain.
I know you have everything in your hand.
And, just across the street you let everything grow
so that at least we do not go hungry.
You are a merciful and good God.
You are the greatest, and you do as you will.
And that is good for all. Amen.

GHANA

▶ The Chief's Prayer

I am sitting here at my desk
and the end of the day surrounds me,
But you are even here, Lord,
and I beg you to bless my work.
Give me strength
so I can do what must be done.
And may it be good.
You also know that I must make decisions,
they are always difficult,
for I must deal with other men.
Make the right decisions plain to them.
Give me a clear head and a warm heart.
Give me your power and humility
to issue orders and regulations,
so that it may be rightly done.
Let me never forget that the workers
are also my brothers and sisters,
and that, in your eyes,
they are worth more than I am.
They have families, honor, feelings, and rights.
Let me never forget that they come first.
I am sure that if you are with me,
my work will succeed.
I ask your help for the welfare of my workers,
    the well-being of all our families and your glory.
Amen.

GHANA

Children

| | | | | | | | |

▶ Keep Watch Over us

O God, turn your ear to hear me.
Protect my children and my cattle, and even if you are weary,
please be patient and listen to my prayer. Under the dark cloak
of night, the splendor of your world sleeps on, invisible to us.
And when your sun moves across the sky each day, I continue
to pray to you. May the spirits of our departed ancestors who
can still exercise their influence on us, keep guard over us, from
their places beyond the earth.

NANDI, KENYA

▶ In Thanksgiving for the Birth of a Child

O Creator,
you who have created
all human beings,
you have conferred
a great benefit on us
by bringing us this child.

KAMBA, KENYA

▶ To Make the Father Known

You who are deathless,
you who do not know death,
you who live always,
you who never feel the cold sleep,
your children have come to gather around you.
O Father, gird up your strength,
penetrate these young initiates with your shadow.
O Father of our race,
O Father who never dies.

FAN, CAMEROON

▶ Blessing of a Child

A child is like a rare bird.
A child is precious like coral.
A child is precious like brass.
You cannot buy a child on the market.
Not for all the money in the world.
The child you can buy for money is a slave.
We may have twenty slaves,
we may have thirty laborers,
only a child brings us joy,
one's child is one's child.
The buttocks of our child are not so flat
that we should tie the beads on another child's hips.
One's child is one's child.
It may have a watery head or a square head,
one's child is one's child.
It is better to leave behind a child
than let the slaves inherit one's house.

One must not rejoice too soon over a child.
Only the one who is buried by his child
is the one who has truly borne a child.
On the day of our death, our hand cannot hold a
    single cowrie.
We need a child to inherit our belongings.

YORUBA, NIGERIA

▶ In Thanksgiving for a Large Family

O God, thanks!
Here are the human beings whom you gave us.
Today we bring you the food that you have given us.
You, my termite heap on which I can lean,
from which come the termites that I eat;
Lord, we thank you; you have given us joy
with the numerous births you have given us.
Nothing of all that we offer you is worthy of you.

PYGMY, ZAIRE

▶ I Offer My Child to You, Lord

To you, the Creator, to you, the powerful,
I offer this fresh bud,
new fruit of the ancient tree.
You are the Master; we are your children.
To you, the Creator, to you, the powerful,
God, I offer this new plant.

PYGMY, ZAIRE

▶ Hush, Child

Hush, child of my mother,
Hush, hush O my mother!
God, who gave you to me,
if only I could meet him,
I would fall on my knees and pray to him.

You came when the moon was shining,
you came when another was rising,
Hush, hush, O child of my mother!
that we share with God,
God who gave you to me,
may he also bring you up for me.

Hush, child of my mother,
you came when God lit the fire,
you came when he was in a generous mood!
Hush, little lamb.
The lion-cub bites (he is not gentle like you).
God who gave you to me,
will find I have lit a fire,
and I will let him warm himself;
I found he was in a generous mood.
Hush, God gave you to me;
Hush, hush, I will pray to you, God,
you will give me cows and little babies.
And then you will give them increase.

RUANDA-URUNDI, BURUNDI

▶ For the Future Leaders of Our Land

We pray, O Lord,
for young people.
For the youth of our land.
For the youth of our church.
It is you who helps them grow
in body, mind, and spirit.
We know they can do nothing without you.
Please, bring these youth into your manhood.
We nag them continuously.
We constantly find something wrong with them.
And yet they are no worse than we were!
You are the true leader of youth.
You know exactly what they need.
They do not need our musty moralizing.
They do not need our "I know better."
They need your commandments and your grace.
Give the youth of the world patience,
obedience, humility, energy, and joy.
Give them a heart full of gladness.
Let them be happy and not negative like we adults are.
Let them do better than we did!
Train them to be the future leaders of our land. Amen.

GHANA

▶ For Good Fortune

O great God, help us, our families,
the men of this town, the people in general,
our pregnant women,
our daughters and our children especially.
May our town progress.
May our land progress.
May our wives not die a mysterious death
and our men not fall from palm trees.
Help to see that all these things do not occur.
O God, help us,
and you, our ancestors,
who gave birth to us long ago,
help us so that we are well-disposed
and have good fortune,
we and our children, especially.

Mende, Sierra Leone

▶ Our Country Needs Us

Lord, we pray for ourselves,
and for the others of this country,
for the youth of Africa, and of the world.
We are awakening and we do not know
if we are strong enough to carry the responsibility
that awaits us.
Our countries are looking to us.
Old people look at us critically.
They scold us and, even worse, think we are silly.
What shall we do?
For we are not yet strong enough.

The older people forget quickly
just how weak they were when young.
We have not yet had any experience,
and we will not be mature enough to be leaders
for a long time.
We come to you, Lord.
You understand us. You have experience.
You know what we must do and how to do it.
You can lead us so that we will be the hope
of our beloved countries.
Help us to contribute our share
to the development of our countries
here in Africa, and beyond.
We want our faith to play its role,
not because it is ours,
but because you are our Father.
Let us be servants to our countries,
the engine in the car
driving towards a good future,
your future, my future, our future.
Remove our fears and misgivings.
We ask you, Lord,
let us be good road signs
that we may lead many people to you.
But, first of all, we must invite them.
And that is the challenge!
But with your Holy Spirit,
and in your Holy name, everything is possible.
Amen.

GHANA

12

Protection and Help

IIIIIIIII

▶ Guard Us From Danger

My God, guard us
in the narrow and deep valleys full of dangers,
and in the plains without end,
and in the fords we cross small or large.
And God said, "All right!"

SAMBURU, KENYA

▶ I Want to Be Close to You, God

My God, place me where I may be held tightly by you. O God,
let me become like a liana, like millet with very many small
grains. God of the mountain of my ancestors, hear me!

May God be favorable to you: be vigorous like a tree that
lasts through the annual blossoming of its shoots.

My God, grant me light for my eyes to see all things.

My God, you who are here and elsewhere, be a God who
sees and hears. And God said, "All right!"

SAMBURU, KENYA

▶ Let Me Find Work

Now I am lying here on my mat, dear God.
The day is over and there was no work.
Still, I am tired.
And yet, you have given us our daily bread,
and the teacher lets the children go to school without paying.
I don't know what they read and write there.
See to it that they learn nothing bad.
And please, if it's possible, let me find work tomorrow;
the children need something to wear.
But I am not grumbling.
Give us all a quiet night and a sound sleep.
Protect us from the mosquitoes and see to it
    that no one is cold.
You are a great, powerful and loving God.
We praise you and pray to you. Amen.

GHANA

▶ We Are Your Sons

O You, Our Father, Father of our tribe,
When the foot in the night
stumbles against the obstacle that shrinks and rears
and bites,
let it be a branch that rears and strikes,
but not one of thy sharp-toothed children,
O Father of the tribe, we are your sons.

SOURCE UNKNOWN

▶ Sacrificial Prayer for Eternal Life

My God, grant us a life without end,
a life that goes on forever.
My God, grant us a life that proceeds in peace.
My God, forgive us.
My God, great heart divine, do not forget us.
God of the abyss, God of the sky,
God look upon us as we invoke you.
My God, do not get annoyed, we pray you.
My God, we cling to you because of our little ones.
My God, think of us for the things we do not know.
God, free us from sins; lead us with good hearts,
and do not place us where there is evil.
God, think of new mothers: those of children
and of animals.
God, grant us a blessed voice to invoke you
night and morning.
God, look on us as we walk in the night
and in the morning.
And God said: "All right!"

SAMBURU, KENYA

▶ Prayer for the Assembly of the Elders

May God answer us.
God, you will save us.
My God, you will guide us.
My God, think of us night and day.
Make us live long like a dark cloud—the long rains.
Make us fragrant like a citron branch that purifies.
Untie the blessed shells of mothers and of children.

God, guard us, and the shepherds together with us.
My God who are surrounded with stars,
with the moon at your navel,
morning of my God that will rise,
hit us with a blessed wind.
Flood us with your waters.
And God said: "All right!"

SAMBURU KENYA

▶ For Protection When Misfortune Strikes

O God, O Master,
O Lord who knows no Lord,
O rich one who knows no poverty,
all-knowing, whose knowledge is not by learning,
king without any rival to your throne,
God of my land, my Lord,
above me, beneath me—
when misfortune strikes,
as trees protect me from the sun,
please keep far away from me this unhappiness.

O God my Lord, you sun of thirty beams.
At the approach of the enemy
do not permit me, your worm, to die on the ground.
For when we see a worm on the earth,
if we wish to, we crush him,
and if we wish, we spare him.
God, who walks with good and evil in your hand,
my Lord, let us not be killed:
for we have begged you!

GALLA, ETHIOPIA

▶ My God, Be by My Side

My God, grant me to walk all roads.
My God, cover me with your black cloak softened by oil.
My God, hold me tight when I walk
and when I stand still.
My God, do not throw me out of you.
My God, keep me in your stomach.
My God, guard me; God answer me.
My God, do not throw me away.
Listen, that we may agree on what I am telling you.
Grant us a life that never ends.
God, answer with favor to what we told you.

SAMBURU, KENYA

▶ Prayer to the Father of Our Fathers

Thou, O God, Father of our fathers,
Let the thundercloud stream!
Let our flocks live!
Let us also live, please!
I am so very weak indeed
from thirst, from hunger!
Let me eat field fruits!
Are you not our Father?
The Father of our fathers?

O that we may praise thee!
That we may bless!
Thou Father of the fathers!
Thou our Lord! Thou, O God!

NAMA, SOUTH AFRICA

▶ Do Not Reject Us

Do not reject us, O God.
Grant us to proceed peacefully, I ask you,
in all places where you have your dwelling.
Hear us.
I ask you for food for our hearts.
Do not get annoyed when we invoke you.
Only to you we turn, to reach the place
where you make us go.
Do not allow me to have difficulties with you,
because it is bad if I have difficulties.

SAMBURU, KENYA

▶ O, Great Spirit

Great Spirit, piler up of rocks into towering mountains! When you stamp on the stone, the dust rises and fills the land. Hardness of the precipice; waters of the flood that turn into misty rain when stirred. Vessel overflowing with oil! Father who sews the heavens like cloth: let him knit together that which is below. Caller-forth of the branching trees, you bring forth the shoots that stand erect. You have filled the land with people; the dust rises on high, O Lord! Wonderful one, you live in the midst of the sheltering rocks. You give rain to humankind. Hear us, O Lord! Show mercy when we beg you, O Lord! You are on high with the spirits of the great. You raise the grass-covered hills above the earth, and create the rivers, Gracious One!

SHONA, ZIMBABWE

▶ For an Understanding of God and an End to Fears

Strong God in heaven,
I do not belong to those
who pray to you on the church hill.
Lord, I do not dare, for my clothes are shabby;
I cannot read or write.
But I know that you are over all gods.
Lord, I know our little idols live on our fears,
I know it, but I fear them nevertheless.

Lord, you are the mighty God of heaven,
the God who provides.
The Christians say that you have given us Jesus Christ.
Lord, I would like to be able to understand this.

Lord, my little idols are not
even as strong as the magician's tricks.
Those tricks are strong; they work in the village
and a little bit along the path.
But you are lord over Kumasi and Accra,
over the ocean and over London.

Lord of Lords, I pray to you
for myself and my family,
for the palm trees from which I draw the wine.
Lord, I wish I had no fear of idols.

Strong God in heaven,
you are Lord as far as I can see—
and here am I, skipping along
with my weaker little prayer.
Mighty God, what you say is coming to pass.

I cannot sacrifice much,
but your people say that you accept even pennies.

I would love to believe in you
and not be afraid of the idols.
Please, please, please! Amen.

GHANA

▶ God, Continue Your Help

God, we pray, help us,
that we may live and continue to have strength;
may we bear children and cattle,
and those who have them
they too say: help our children.

MERU, KENYA

▶ For Success

My father built, and his father built,
and I have built.
Leave me to live here in success,
let me sleep in comfort, and have children.
There is food for you.

BANYORO, UGANDA

▶ God, Take Care of My Needs

My God, do not throw me away. God, I have invoked you. My God, be listening from your heights, and raise us up towards you. My God be the one who is always around on the earth. Do not forget me. Help me to avoid the charge of an elephant, and may I roar like a lion.

My God, please listen, no matter how I talk to you. God, help me to last like the hump of a camel. My God, make me as solid as a mountain. God, be agreeable, so that the rain may not dry up, and that there may always be water. God, I have asked for your salvation.

God, keep me safe every morning and every evening. And at night, place me where you have placed your stars. Surround me with a blessed life. Help me to carry on in calmness, a life without stops. My God, help me to carry on with my life as a witness and a sacrifice.

My God, I have begged you; I have turned to you. My God, do not reject me, be agreeable. My God, take care of me when I go through a winding road; my God, I shall avoid a winding road—let me go along a straight road only. My God, help me to meet life; I am in danger of getting lost.

My God, I do not know what I am doing; I follow you alone, because you alone know what has to be done. You know what I shall do. My God, I have annoyed you and I stand before you now. Since the time I came, I have been begging you; God, be my God. Be the God of all.

O God, be the God of the cattle. Guard each animal as it is grazing; watch over it as it rests. My God, be watchful. Help the cattle to find grass which is still sweet. And may they drink sweet water. God, may they quench their thirst with sweet water.

O God, send the great black cloud of rain; let it not vanish like smoke. O God, be agreeable.

SAMBURU, KENYA

▶ God, You Are the Source of Life

O God of our forebears, all our lives depend on you, and without you we are nothing. It is you who look after wealth; give us plenty of good harvest, rain, and wealth and children. Without you we can't live because we shall have no food or water to drink. You are the source of life. You protected us on our journey to this fertile land. Where we came from, we don't know, but you know. You are the God of wars and fights. Protect us against anyone who wants to harm us, especially here at my home.

ADHOLA, UGANDA

▶ May God Grant What You Desire

God, be a safeguard to all things.
May God grant you the best of fragrances,
	so that you may be fragrant with life.
May God grant you all you desire.
May God make you reach everything that you know
	or don't know.
My God, watch over us now. And God said: "All right."

SAMBURU, KENYA

▶ God, Make Me Walk in Peace

God, grant that your fruits
be our fragrance.
My God, may they not cease
to be fragrant.
My God, let your life
be my fragrance,
my God, forever, all my days.
My God, make me walk in peace;
may I walk in peace every day.
My God, I have prayed you
to grant me a long life without jolts,
like things carried by calm waters.
My God, grant that I may be like
things carried by water.
And God said, "All right."

SAMBURU, KENYA

▶ I Turn to You, Father

O Father, Creator, God, I ask your help!
I invoke you, O my Father!
To you, Father, I turn.

Come, everyone, and beg God to give life to humankind,
come, everyone and receive life from God.
Rain mixed with sunbeams will give us life.
Ask life for the flocks, the herds, and the people
Sacrifice the white ox, so that God may come closer,
so that the Father may give us life.

Now, let us reunite;
the Father has life to give;
the great Man has life.
O Father, Creator come!
We are reunited.
Give life to herds, to flocks and to people.
O Father, come!

DINKA, SUDAN

▶ Our Lord, Our Moon

May you be for us a moon of joy and happiness. Let the young become strong and the grown man maintain his strength, the pregnant women be delivered and the woman who has given birth suckle her child. Let the stranger come to the end of his journey and those who remain at home dwell safely in their houses. Let the flocks that go to feed in the pastures return happily. May you be a moon of harvest and of calves. May you be a moon of restoration and of good health.

MENSA, ETHIOPIA

▶ Guard This Homestead

You, the Great Elder, who dwells on the Kere-Nyaga,
your blessing allows homesteads to spread.
Your anger destroys homesteads.
We beseech you, and in this we are in harmony
with the spirits of our ancestors:
we ask you to guard this homestead and let it spread.
Let the women, the herds and flocks be plentiful
Chorus Peace; praise ye God. Peace be with us.

KIKUYU, KENYA

▶ Guard Our Group

My God, turn your attention to us.
I invoke you, my God, under a shady tree.
My God, look upon our group; remember your group.
My God, hear us. My God, guard our group.
My God, don't get tired; guard us; do not forget your group.
Put us back into our place; give us your blessings.
My God, be the support of our group and of us who are
    here,
and grant us a life of perpetual tranquillity.
God, grant to the group a blessed life.
May it be so, my God.

SAMBURU, KENYA

▶ Let the Wound Heal

Friend, God, who is in this village,
as you are very great we tell you about this wound.
For you are the God of our home, in very truth.
We tell you about the fight of this lad:
let the wound heal, let it be ransomed.

NUER, SUDAN

13

Reconciliation and Forgiveness

||||||||||

▶ Prayer of General Confession

God, we have come before you to worship,
and to confess our sins which we have done during the week.
> Response: May They All Go Away.

We have sinned before thee in speaking to people,
we have offended thy creatures, we have spoken bad words,
we have grieved their hearts, O God.
> Response: May They All Go Away.

Our Chiefs do not love one another in their hearts.
Take such hearts from them and give them one heart.
> Response: May They All Go Away.

A new commandment you have given unto us all
to love one another as in heaven where
> there is no quarreling.
Teach us to keep your word, O God.
> Response: May They All Go Away.

That our Chiefs may be one in loving
and ruling their country and their people, and lead us well.
This we pray, God, grant us.

> Response: May They All Go Away.

Africa is the land of our ancestors.
We have changed her with our new ways,
by leaving all the ways of our ancestors,
ways which gave peace to the country, O God.

> Response: May They All Go Away.

Our Church is calling everyone to come in
so that the house of marriage may be filled.
It is thy work to give them all new dresses.

> Response: May They All Go Away.

We are taking beer as wild animals;
we forget worship which is our life.
Teach us to drink beer moderately, O God.

> Response: May They All Go Away.

Creator, Son and Holy Spirit,
one God ever and ever.
Amen. Amen. Amen.

NYAKYUSA, TANZANIA

▶ For My Son

Ah God, you know this is my son; I begot him and trained him and labored for him, and now that he should do some work for me, he refuses. In anything he now does in the world, may he not prosper until he comes back to me and begs my pardon....

Ah God, this is my son. He left me without any good fortune in the world, because he knows I have cursed him. He has now come back to beg me to revoke the curse, as I am doing now. Wherever he goes now, may he prosper and have many children.

MENDE, SIERRA LEONE

▶ Satan's Departure

God in Heaven, you have helped my life to grow like a tree. Now something has happened. Satan, like a bird, has carried in one twig of his own choosing after another. Before I knew it, he had built a dwelling place and was living in it. Tonight, my Father, I am throwing out both the bird and the nest.

NIGERIA

||| 14 |||

Journeys and Meetings

||||||||

▶ Before a Journey

May God carry you.
Mount on God's camel that does not rock.
May God be with you, at your right and at your left.
May God lead you ahead.
Look without being seen.
May God hide you and put you into God's own secret place,
that you may be invisible.
Find salvation.
True is the heart of children, mothers and cattle.
Rest peacefully in the land where you shall go,
a blessed land.
Do not bow your head in sorrow.
May God hide you from dangers
also in the open spaces without shelter.
May God place you where our creator places the stars
of the morning.
And God said: "All right."

SAMBURU, KENYA

▶ So That I Return Safe and Sound

O grandfather, today I am going on a journey, a very long journey. Help me on the road that I am going to take, so that I will walk without stumbling throughout the voyage. A man travels towards his neighbors with a joyful heart. May the wicked man remain with his wickedness. May all unhappiness stay to one side of me, so that I may return safe and sound. And you, our God, kindly guard me and keep me safe on the road I follow. Let me walk without stumbling. May every unhappiness that you have made, be directed towards another place. Look kindly on me so that at my return, cries of joy will resound: Olo! Olo!

TUTSHIOKWÉ, CONGO

▶ Returning From a Journey

O Grandfather, see, I went on a journey, and I did not see any misfortune, and I went without stumbling. Indeed you listened to my prayer, I will pay honor to you. I returned from the place to which I went, and with good things. Now you, you can take your reward. I thank you; thank you very much indeed.

TUTSHIOKWÉ, CONGO

▶ Before a Meeting

My God, who is in all things,
rise up from the abyss.
My God, enable us to agree
both in the morning and in the evening.
My God, breathe upon us
with your blessed breath,
and, my God, answer to what I have said.
And God said: "All right."

SAMBURU, KENYA

▶ Let God Shield You

Now you depart, and though your way may lead
through airless forests thick with *hhagar* trees,
places steeped in heat, stifling and dry,
where breath comes hard, and no fresh breeze can reach—
yet may God place a shield of coolest air
between your body and the assailant sun.

And in a random scorching flame of wind
that parches the painful throat and sears the flesh,
may God, in compassion, let you find
the great-boughed tree that will protect and shade.

On every side of you, I now would place
prayers from the holy book, to bless your path,
that ills may not descend, nor evils harm,
and you may travel in the peace of faith.

To all the blessings I bestow on you,
friend, yourself now say the last "amen."

SOMALI, SOMALIA

⫟15⫟ Marriage

||||||||

▶ For a Bride

Meet life; meet it together with your children.
Meet it blessed, meet it near, meet it far,
the distance from south to north.
Untie your blessed shells; be a majestic tree,
refreshing to the travelers.
Spread out like palm leaves.
May God grant you children;
may God grant you many of them,
that your food may not be sufficient.
Spread out like the water of a lake.
May you be loved by the generation now living,
and by the one that is no more.
May children call you "grandma."
Be an ant-hill on which children play.
Be the hinge of your door that does not fail.
May you nourish all nine generations.
Together with your axe, with numerous offspring
like a millipede's legs, go now,
for God has agreed.

SAMBURU, KENYA

▶ May God Enlarge Everything That Is Yours

Start your walk towards the place where God wants you.
May God enlarge your sleeping mat; may God enlarge
the door of your dwelling; may God enlarge your back.
May God lead you by pulling you along,
and may God push you.
May God be at your side.
May God grant you many children.
May God grant you many cattle.
Spread out, like water of a lake. May God be your deliverer.
I have placed myself in front of you to lead you.
Be like a powerful tree, with a refreshing shadow.
Give us life.
Go without stopping.

SAMBURU, KENYA

▶ May God Watch Over You

May God free you, may God guard you night and day.
May God set you in your right place, and may you
spread out like the grass of a prairie.
Spread out like palm leaves; continue your walk,
and may life be with you.
May God place you where God's stars are placed
at dawn and at night.
Spread out like water of a lake.
Be numerous like the feet of a millipede.

SAMBURU, KENYA

16

Sickness and Health, Aging and Suffering, Death and Burial

||||||||

▶ To Remove Suffering

God—owner of all things,
I pray you, give me what I need,
because I am suffering,
and also my children are suffering
and all things that are in this country of mine.
I beg thee for life,
the good one with things,
healthy people with no disease,
may they bear healthy children.
And also to women who suffer because they are barren,
open the way by which they may see children.
Give goats, cattle, food, honey.
And also the troubles of the other lands
that I do not know, remove.

MERU, KENYA

▶ Give Us Health

God! give us health,
and that it may be given to us, strength
and that it may be given to us, milk.
If any man eats it, may he like it.
If the pregnant woman eats it, may she like it.

NANDI, KENYA

▶ Give Us Rain

God give us rain
and we, thy people, shall be well;
we shall be well with health;
that is sweet.

SUK, KENYA

▶ Let Us Walk in Health

You Divinity, we shall kill your ox,
and better that you should be pleased with us.
You will let us walk in health,
and we have made a feast so that there should be no fever,
and that no other illnesses should seize people,
that they may all be well.
And if my clansman travels,
then let him complete his journey without sickness,
and let no evil befall him or anybody.
And you, Divinity, do not bring evil upon us,
and I shall be pleased.
You women, clap your hands and sing.
And woo away the fever, that nothing may be wrong with us.
You, tribe of my father, walk in health,

nothing shall harm us, and Divinity will be pleased with us,
and we will pray to Divinity
that there may be no bad things,
and sing.

DINKA, SUDAN

▶ Forgive Our Unintentional Sins

My God, may your answer bring us life
that proceeds calmly and surpasses the mountain-tops
May it be a life of respite for us,
since you are a savior who saves us all.
You save us through good fortune
in the evil we have committed.
Forgive us what we have done,
because, God, we do not know what we did,
and it was without any intention of doing evil.
We do not know what path we have walked through.
If we knew it, we would not have done it.
If it were anything obvious for all,
we would not have done it.
When we answer you, God, in a certain way,
know that it happens as I have said.
My God, forgive us that evil which is unintentional.
Let it be so, my God.
Restore all our hearts, so that
we may follow your goodness.
By means of your strength remove from us
the evil that is within our hearts.
God, answer!
Yes! God has answered.

SAMBURU, KENYA

▶ For a Peaceful Death for My Mother

Slowly the muddy pool becomes a river
slowly my mother's disease becomes death.
When wood breaks, it can be repaired.
But ivory breaks forever.
An egg falls to reveal a messy secret.
My mother went and carried her secret along.
She has gone far—we look for her in vain.
But when you see the Kob antelope on the way to the farm,
when you see the Kob antelope on the way to the river—
leave your arrows in the quiver,
and let the dead depart in peace.

YORUBA, NIGERIA

▶ Grant Us Prosperity

My God, do not take away anything else from us;
my God, leave to us the good of our bodies.
My God, make us overflow with life;
my God, give us a life of prosperity;
make us prosper on earth, my God.
God, grant us continuity,
to prosper in all things
and in all you give us.
My God, listen to what I told you.
And God said: "All right."

SAMBURU, KENYA

▶ Save Me From Ruin, Lord

God, Supreme Being,
here I am, very unhappy,
for all my possessions are scattered at random.
My family and my heart are completely overturned.
I who have never committed theft,
my possessions here are the property of all my family;
they are the things inherited from my ancestors.
All people have goods which coexist with them in peace
but my house is as if consumed by fire.
My God, you arrange all the affairs of men and women;
I have kept all the rules; everything is useless.
Now it's up to you, God.
Why not strike down the person who has a grudge against me?
My goods and my neighbors, all of us
belong to you, God.
You, Sun that we are unable to look at directly,
you, life force, my misery overflows.
I, who never seduced the wife of another man,
who have never taken another man's goods by force,
who is jealous of no one; I am ruined.
Everyone else has possessions which prosper;
my own possessions evaporate on all sides,
and are always getting lost.
God, Supreme Being, Sun that we cannot look upon directly,
I am running headlong to my ruin, with all that I have.
Even sleep deserts me in my own house.
May the person who bears me a grudge suffer misfortune!
May the one emboldened to shout:
"I wish nothing good to this man";
may that one be jeered at and mocked in public.

BALUBA, CONGO

Sickness and Health, Aging and Suffering, Death and Burial ● 87

▶ For a Long and Fruitful Life

My God, do not take away from me this fresh water.
My God, grant me to quench my thirst again with this water.
My God, morning of my God, rise over us in peace.
God of the mountain of our fathers,
my God, I have prayed to you.
Do not come with bad things.
My God, grant me to proceed tranquilly,
as long as I hold the staff of my authority.
My God, allow me to reach an old age without end,
and grant that I might be covered by you and my
children with blessed leaves.
And may I be buried by the children of my son,
and may they call me grandfather or grandmother.
When I die, do not allow any children to be distressed.
When I am dying, my son, do not allow a beast to eat me.
When I fall asleep forever, let me lie down in the best
way so that God may help you.
Never show evil to God.
When I die, place me in a grave:
dig a deep grave within the cattle enclosure:
bury me within the enclosure of our cattle.
If you do so, God will help you;
truly so, my son.

SAMBURU, KENYA

▶ Help Us Through This Sickness

You, Father God,
who are in the heavens and below;
creator of everything and understanding everything;

maker of the earth and of the heaven—
we are but little children unknowing anything evil.
If this sickness has been brought by a person
we beg you, help us through these roots.
In case it was inflicted by you, the Conserver,
likewise we beg your mercy on your child.
Also you, our grandparents, who sleep in the place
of the shades, we beg all of you,
help us in this trouble, have compassion on us,
so that we can sleep peacefully.
And so I spit out this mouthful of water!
Pu-pu! Pu-pu!
Please listen to our earnest request.

LUGURU, TANZANIA

▶ A Peaceful Death

Let us behave gently,
that we may die peacefully;
That our children may stretch out their hands
upon us in burial.

YORUBA, NIGERIA

▶ May We Not Die Young

That we may not die young;
that we may not attain an old age of wretchedness;
that we may not scratch the ground with a stick
in the place of sacrifices.

YORUBA, NIGERIA

▶ God, Be My Relief

God, agree with us; wake up.
God, watch; my God be my relief.
May God relieve me of this disease of mine.
God, give me your medicine,
your blessed medicine that does not die or end.
Grant a lasting life that may not run away while we live.
Grant a life that does not stop.
Grant a strong heart;
grant what comes on a blessed night,
that we may always find it while we live.
Grant a blessed voice that may be heard continually,
like a blessed bell.
Listen to it when you sleep and when you walk.
May God grant you a strong heart that does not break,
that lasts forever.

SAMBURU, KENYA

▶ For a Quick Recovery

Brightness, help this man that he may be well,
that he may recover tomorrow,
and may you want to help this man to be well;
and, as overcoming you overcame,
overcome all these troubles,
and have mercy on me,
because we do not know how to pray to God
differently from what we say now.

MERU, KENYA

▶ To Always Be in Good Health

May we be in good health always;
remove all misfortunes from us.
May sickness be gone;
may poverty be gone;
may death be gone;
instead, may abundant life be ours forever.
Provide the necessary protection for all members
         of the lineage,
in the same way as they have all gathered to honor you today.
May all members of the public be kind to us.
Give us success when we go to farm;
give us success when we go to fish;
give us success when we go to trade.
O venerable one, abundant life and prosperity for all of us.

ANLO EWE, GHANA

▶ Sorrow

As for me, God has devoured me.
As for me God has not dealt with me as with others.
With singing I would sing
if only my dead brother were with me.
Sorrow is not to hang the head in mourning,
sorrow is not to go weeping—to weep will not
      remove sorrow.
As for me, God has devoured me.
If God had dealt with me as with others
I could be the "scorner-of-enemies."
Woe is me!

RUANDA-URUNDI, BURUNDI

▶ To Walk Along a Good Road

God has answered
to the words we told him,
and we have answered
to God's words,
so that when we die
God may put us in a good place,
as we do not know what happens
when one dies.
So, we pray to God every day.
Keep away from unjust curses,
because we do not know God's words,
because God loves a good speech,
and because God is pleased if we walk
along a good road.

SAMBURU, KENYA

▶ Prayer for a Journey

In your journeys to and fro
God direct thee;
In your happiness and pleasure
God bless thee;
In care, anxiety, or trouble
God sustain thee;
In peril and in danger
God protect thee.

TIMOTHY OLUFOYSOYE, NIGERIA

▶ Father, Thank You

Father, thank you for your revelation
about death, and illness, and sorrow.

Thank you for speaking so plainly to us,
for calling us all friends and hovering over us;
for extending your arms out to us.

We cannot stand on our own;
we fall into death without you.
We fall from faith, left to our own.
We are really friendless without you.

Your extended arms fill us with joy,
expressing love, asking and receiving our trust.

You have our trust, Father, and our faith,
with our bodies and all that we are and possess.

We fear nothing when we are with you,
we are safe to stretch out and help others,
those troubled in faith, those troubled in body.

Father, help us to do with our bodies what we proclaim,
that our faith be known to you and to others,
and be effective in all the world.

MAASAI, TANZANIA

17

Night Prayers

IIIIIIII

▶ Watch Over Us While We Sleep

God, save us. God, hide us.
When we sleep, God do not sleep.
If we sleep, God do not get drowsy.
Tie us around your arm, God,
like a bracelet.
Guard us now, my God, guard us and save us.
God, guard for us our little ones
both people and beasts, whether awake or asleep.
God, look on us with a countenance that is happy.
Hit us with the black cloud of rain like the long rains.
God, give us your waters.
God, give us what we ardently desire in regards to children,
and to cattle.
God, do not make our land barren.
God, give us places where there is life.
God, divide us fairly into dead and alive.
And God said: "All right."

SAMBURU, KENYA

▶ Be Our Support

My God, turn your thoughts to us;
do not reject us.
Stars of my God, moon of my God, be our support.
Grant us nourishment. Be our support.
Grant us life in cattle and children.
God, grant us what is desired.
Horn-of-my-buffalo be our support.
White fleece of all riches,
my breast, grant us what is desired,
and grant us what does not end.
My God, founder of my family,
my creator who is in the skies, be our support.
My God, do not reject me,
because I shall not reject you.
Remember me when I sleep and when I walk.
My God, give me rain.
Turn your thoughts to our children.
Turn your thoughts to our cattle.
My God, be my support.

SAMBURU, KENYA

▶ For a Peaceful Night

O God, you have let me pass this day in peace,
let me pass the night in peace
O Lord who has no Lord,
there is no strength but in thee.
Thou alone hast no obligation.
Under thy hand I pass the night.
Thou art my mother and my father.

BORAN, KENYA

▶ I Turn to God in Prayer

Now that evening has fallen,
to God the Creator will I turn in prayer,
knowing that God will help me.
I know the Creator will help me.

DINKA, SUDAN

▶ May We Sleep in Peace

God, grant that we might sleep in peace in this hut;
and that at the break of day
we may find ourselves in safety.

DIOLA, CAMEROON

▶ For God's Grace

Come, Lord,
and cover me with the night.
Spread your grace over us
as you assured us you would do.

Your promises are more than
all the stars in the sky;
your mercy is deeper than the night.
Lord, it will be cold.
The night comes with its breath of death.
Night comes; the end comes; you come.
Lord, we wait for you day and night.

GHANA

▶ To Treat Matters With Careful Consideration

Let us not run the world hastily;
let us not grasp at the rope of wealth impatiently;
what should be treated with mature judgment
let us not treat in a fit of temper.
Whenever we arrive at a cool place
let us rest sufficiently well.
Let us give prolonged attention to the future,
and then let us give due regard to
the consequences of things,
and that is on account of our sleeping.

YORUBA, NIGERIA

▶ Help Me Sleep Well

Lord, you are the Lord, help me sleep well,
so that I may get up tomorrow with my limbs healthy;
and show me the work I have to do.

MERU, KENYA

▶ A Night Prayer

I implore you, God,
I pray to you during the night.
How are all people kept by you all days?
And you walk in the midst of the grass,
I walk with you;
when I sleep in the house I sleep with you.
To you I pray for food, and you give it to the people
and water to drink.

SHILLUK, SUDAN

▶ Watch Over Us As We Sleep

God, be watchful; watch over us now.
My God, answer favorably what I ask you.
Do not get tired, but keep awake and watch over us.
Pasture all creatures everywhere.
Do not rest; provide a shepherd of the night and of the day.
Do not throw us away; support us by our armpits.
Watch over us and look upon us a lot.

Provide stars continually for the night
        and for the day.
Place us where the stars are.
Move around with your blessed swarm—the Milky Way—
where our cows are, and our goats and sheep.
Be watchful where mothers are, and elders.
Place fertility where our young brides are
and our cows and our sheep.

My God, do not do any evil to us.
My God, guard our shepherds. Guard our cattle.
Guard and watch over those who can see and those
who do not have eyes, because they are all poor:
the one who has eyesight is also poor:
both the one who has and the one who has not—
watch over them all.

God, watch over everybody,
over those who live and those who don't.
Watch over all, over children who are born
and over those who are not born,
and over those still in the womb.
God, watch over all of them, and over all others too.

Protect everybody who is here, and those who are not.
God, guard our children, those who are far or near.
Watch over far places and near ones.
Guide all our children, that they may get home.
My God, watch over and protect
all our children and all our lands.

My God, give us life year after year,
that I may master a long life
and advance into old age.
May God grant what is desired.

SAMBURU, KENYA

▶ I Am Not Afraid

The sun has disappeared.
I have switched off the light.
And my wife and children are asleep.
The animals in the forest are full of fear,
as are the people on their mats.
They prefer the day with your sun to the night.
But I still know that your moon is there,
and your eyes, and also your hands.
Thus I am not afraid.
This day again you led us wonderfully.
Everybody went to his mat satisfied and full.
Renew us during our sleep,
that in the morning we may come afresh to our daily jobs.
Be with our brothers far away who may just be getting up
    now. Amen.

GHANA

⫸ 18 ⫷

More African Prayers

||||||||||

In this final chapter, we have included additional prayers by Africans—from Saint Augustine to Desmond Tutu—as well as intercessory prayers addressed to African saints. This is, by no means, an exhaustive list.

▶ For Courage in the Face of Danger

Martyrs of Uganda, pray for faith when and where it is in danger. Pray for all Christians who suffer because of their faith. Grant them the same courage, joy and love you showed. Help those who live in zones of war and destruction, places where Christianity is not accepted. Help those of us who live in the freedoms of faith remember your struggles and those continuing to this very day for the defense of the faith. May persecutions of all kinds end in the world! Amen.

SAINT CHARLES LWANGA (D. 1886) AND COMPANIONS

Charles Lwanga and twenty-two others were martyred for their faith by King Mwanga of Uganda in 1887.

▶ To Restore Harmony

Father, you are the origin of all that is holy, you are true goodness, you are true justice. Through you, we find peace, harmony, and serenity. Heal all that separates us from each other and you, restore harmony in our lives, unite us in love. May love unite us with your Holy Spirit so that all is peaceful again. We make this request through the mercy, compassion, and grace of Jesus Christ, your only Son. Amen.

SAINT DIONYSIUS OF ALEXANDRIA, C. 200 –C. 265

Exiled from Alexandria in Egypt twice by Roman persecutions, Dionysius the Great (as Saint Basil referred to him) was a staunch defender of the faith, a learned teacher, and active in church affairs as the Bishop of Alexandria for 17 years.

▶ For Peace

O merciful Lord, you who are so exalted, you are peace, love, kindness, purity, and goodness. Make us worthy of your peace. We are meek and filled with love for you and our spiritual brothers. May we embrace one another in spirit and the perfection of your divine love so we may seek the fulfillment of your commandment. This way, we will become your children in love, peace, and tranquility, and finally, be worthy to receive your divine blessings, just as your only Son promised. Praise be peace, may it reign through your Holy Spirit, now and forever more. Amen.

SAINT CYRIL OF ALEXANDRIA, 370–444

Bishop and Patriarch of Alexandria, Saint Cyril fought against the Nestorian heresy. He is a Doctor of the Church.

▶ In Thanksgiving and Joy

O Mary, Mother of God, Mother of the Church, thanks to you, at the dawn of the Annunciation, the whole human race with its cultures, rejoiced in knowing itself capable of the Gospel. On this eve of a new Pentecost for the Church of Africa, Madagascar and the Islands, together with the people entrusted to us, in communion with the Holy Father, we unite ourselves to you, so that the outpouring of the Holy Spirit may make our cultures places of communion in diversity, and may make us the Church—Family of the Father, the Brotherhood of the Son, the image of the Trinity, anticipating the Reign of God and working with all for a society that has God as its Builder, a society of Justice and of Peace. Amen!

ROMAN CATHOLIC BISHOPS FOR AFRICA

From the Apostolic Exhortation "Ecclesia in Africa," issued for the African synod held April 11 to May 8, 1994.

▶ To End All Persecutions

O Eternal Word, Son of God, hear my prayer for clemency!

End all persecutions in your faithful. Grant courage to those who are subject to these trials, strengthen them in you!

End the persecutions of your people! Amen.

SAINT PETER OF ALEXANDRIA, D. 311

Born at Alexandria, Saint Peter was martyred in 311 under Emperor Maximinus Daia. As bishop, he tolerantly welcomed back those Christians who had apostatized. Peter is thought to be the last Christian to die for the faith before Constantine granted religious toleration throughout the empire.

▶ Prayer for Peace and Brotherhood

After the crucifixion of my country for over four hundred years, Lord, hear my prayer of peace and forgiveness!

Lord God, forgive the white slave-traders of Europe and over the seas! They hunted my children like wild elephants. They caught them, tied them up, whipped them and soiled their hands with their blood.

Forgive those who exported tens of millions of my sons and daughters. They left my forests barren. My eyes are so filled with tears–they turn to ice at the very thought of these acts of hatred. The serpent of hate arises in my heart—a serpent I long ago thought had disappeared. Destroy that serpent, Lord.

Bless my people, Lord, those who seek their own faces under the threat of being recognized. May they continue to seek you in spite of the cold and famine that eats at their very bones, at their very insides. The woman who laments her absent husband, the fiancée her lost love, the mother her dead son, bless those who have lost loved ones, may we all unite under your love.

With your help, may all of the people of Europe, Asia, Africa, and all who have sweated blood and suffering look beyond that and see the haloed heads of my people. Extend a warm handshake to them so that we may all interlace our fingers to belt the earth in fraternal love. Amen.

LÉOPOLD SÉDAR SENGHOR, 1906–

Poet, politician, and philosopher, Léopold Sédar Senghor was president of Senegal from 1960 to 1981.

▶ For Mercy

Late, late have I known you, O ancient truth! Late have I loved you. O beauty ever ancient and ever new! And behold, you are within, and I was wandering outside, and there I sought you, and, deformed as I was, I ran after those beautiful things which you have created.

You were with me and I was not with you. Those things kept me far from you, those things which could have no being but in you.

You have called. You have cried out. You have pierced my deafness and dispersed my blindness. You have sent forth Your Fragrance and I have drawn my breath, and now I long for you, and hunger after you.

Now my hope is nothing else but in your boundless mercy, O Lord, my God. He who loves you, loves you for your own sake and not for anything else. O love, ever burning and never extinguished, true charity; my God, set me afire! Give me what you command and command what you will. Amen.

SAINT AUGUSTINE, 354–430

One of the greatest theologians of Christianity and a diligent and effective critic of the heresies of the early Church. Augustine was born in 354 in North Africa of a Christian mother and a pagan father. After an early life of self-indulgence, Augustine converted to Christianity in 386, and was made Bishop of Hippo. His most famous works include The City of God, On the Trinity, *and his* Confessions, *the story of his early life.*

▶ An Instrument of Peace

Make me, O Lord, the instrument of your love, that I may bring comfort to those who sorrow and joy to those who are regarded as persons of little account. In this country of many races make me courteous to those who are humble and understanding to those who are resentful. Teach me what I should be to the arrogant, the cruel, for I do not know.

And as for me myself, make me more joyful than I am, especially if this is needed for the sake of others. Let me remember my many experiences of joy and thankfulness. And may I this coming day do some work of peace for thee.

ALAN STEWART PATON, SOUTH AFRICA

Author of Cry the Beloved Country, *Alan Paton opposed the apartheid of his native South Africa. This prayer was a favorite of Mother Teresa of Calcutta.*

▶ My Feet Are Dirty

O Jesus, my feet are dirty. Come even as a slave to me, pour water into your bowl, come and wash my feet. In asking such a thing I know I am overly bold, but I dread what was threatened when you said, "If I do not wash your feet I have no fellowship with you." Wash my feet, then, because I long for your companionship. Though you wash me now, I shall still stand in need of that other washing, the cleansing of your baptism.

ORIGEN OF ALEXANDRIA, 182-250

Distinguished Father of the early Church, Origen was a teacher, writer, and scriptural scholar. He was tortured to death under Emperor Maximinus.

▶ For Courage and Hope for Eternal Life

Lord, grant me the strength and courage to endure what I must. Lord, help me put all of my hope in you for the gift of eternal life at the end of my road. Give me life beyond the death of my body! Amen.

SAINT SATURNINUS, D. 304

African martyr tortured to death along with his four children and other members of his family for their determination to celebrate the Eucharist.

▶ For Truth in All Things

God of all Truth, we ask you to teach us what is true. May we only know your Truth and keep it holy. If we have been harboring untruths, correct us, set us on the right path. If we fall, may your Truth help us up. Keep us away from those things that will harm our understanding of your Truth. May we always live in truth, your Truth. We ask this in the name of your true Son, Jesus Christ. Amen.

SAINT FULGENTIUS OF RUSPE, 467–533

Born near Carthage, Fulgentius entered a monastery at the age of twenty-two. In 507 he was elected bishop of Ruspe (Tunisia) against his will, and was almost immediately banished to Sardinia. During his exile, Fulgentius devoted his time to writing against the Arian heresy. He returned to his see in 532 and died there in 533.

▶ To Love the Lord and Have Compassion for Others Like Saint Josephine Bakhita

O Holy Trinity, when I see the sun, moon, and stars, I say: "Who created these beautiful things?" I want to see him, know him and give thanks for his bountiful gifts.

I give my all to this Master, he will take care of me. I must trust in his knowledge of what is best for me!

I have been baptized with such joy! Only the angels could repeat this story!

If I could only have told my people of your love, I would have won so many souls for you. If I could meet those slave-traders who captured and tortured me, I would kiss their hands and kneel in thanksgiving before them! For, if they had not taken me, I would not now be a Christian! I would not have had a chance to know and love you, my Lord!

You love me so much, you love all your children...we must love you and each other!

You have blessed me with a miracle—I did not die, for I enjoy eternal life with you, I am doing greater things in your holy name!

I was not afraid to die to the earthly life, for that just brought me closer to you. I am a freed slave. I am a child of God! Amen.

SUDAN

Blessed Josephine Bakhita (1869–1947) was kidnaped into slavery and later was sold to an Italian diplomat who took her to Italy where she gained her freedom and joined the Canossian Sisters. She died in 1947.

▶ Prayer for the Sick

Lord, watch over those who sit vigil over the sick tonight, those who weep for others, send your angels to watch over those who sleep.

> Care for the sick, O Lord.
> Give rest to the tired.
> Bless those who are dying.
> Give relief to the sufferers.
> Deem to pity those who are afflicted.
> Protect the joyous.
> Do this, my Lord, out of your love for your children.
> Amen.
>
> *SAINT AUGUSTINE*

▶ In God's Service

Father, you called me to give up all that belonged to the world to follow you, serve you, in solitude in the desert. Through prayer and deed, may I lead others to deny created things and love you above all. May we all be led to practice self-denial and love you alone. Amen.

SAINT ANTONY THE ABBOT, C. 251–356

Father of Christian monasticism, Antony gave away the fortune that had been left to him by his parents, and went to live the life of a hermit in various spots in Lower Egypt. He ate only bread and water and wore only sackcloth and sheepskin. Antony attracted many followers so that he was forced to organize loose colonies of monks in the deserts of the Nile.

▶ The Nativity

Within a simple hut, ere stirred the dawn,
Unto the Pure One was an Infant born,
Wrapped in blue lappah that his mother dyed,
Laid on his father's home-tanned deerskin hide,
The Babe still slept, by all things glorified.
Spirits of black bards burst their bonds and sang
"Peace upon earth" until the heavens rang.
All the black infants who from earth had fled
Peeped through the clouds—then gathered round his head,
Telling of things a baby needs to do,
When first he opens his eyes on wonder new;
Telling him that sleep was sweetest rest,
All comfort came from his black mother's breast,
Their gift was Love, caught from the springing sod,
Then all the Wise Men of the past stood forth,
Filling the air, East, West, and South and North,
And told him of the joy that wisdom brings
To mortals in their earthly wanderings.
The children of the past shook down each bough,
Wreathed frangipani blossoms for his brow,
They put pink lilies in his mother's hand,
And heaped for both the first fruits of the land.
His father cut some palm fronds, that the air
Be coaxed to zephyrs while he rested there.
Birds trilled their hallelujahs; all the dew
Trembled with laughter, till the Babe laughed too.
Black women brought their love so wise,
And kissed their motherhood into his mother's eyes.

AFRICA

Collected by Langston Hughes

▶ Lift Our Hearts

Lord of the spring time, Father of flower, field and fruit, smile on us in these earnest days when the work is heavy and the toil wearisome; lift up our hearts, O God, to the things worthwhile: sunshine and night, the dripping rain, the song of birds, books and music, and the voices of our friends. Lift up our hearts to these this night, O Father, and grant us Thy peace. Amen.

W. E. B. DU BOIS, UNITED STATES/GHANA, 1868–1963

Sociologist and historian, W. E. B. Du Bois was born in Massachusetts and educated at Fisk and Harvard universities. His research into the plight of Black Americans led to his participation in the formation of the National Association for the Advancement of Colored People. After working for that cause, he left to teach at Atlanta University. After World War II, Du Bois became involved in the peace movement and was targeted for harassment by the FBI and the U.S. Justice Department. Finally, he moved to the West African nation of Ghana, where he became a citizen shortly before his ninety-fifth birthday.

▶ Victory Is Ours

Goodness is stronger than evil;
Love is stronger than darkness;
Life is stronger than death;
Victory is ours through Him who loves us.

DESMOND TUTU, 1931–

African clergyman, civil rights activist, and Nobel laureate, Archbishop Tutu is the titular head of the Anglican church in South Africa and was appointed to head of the Truth and Reconciliation Commission called to investigate and collect testimony on human rights violations and other crimes that occurred in South Africa during the period from 1960 to 1996.

▶ For Prisoners and Corrections Officers

Most gracious Father, grant your special blessings to those who are incarcerated. Give them your loving pity. Guide and protect those who have been given a second chance in the world. Grant them forgiveness for their sins and give them strength to start new lives. Lead them on the right path so that with the help of your Holy Spirit, they may stay on the right side of the law and fight against evil in all forms.

Bless those who watch over your children who have erred. Bless the guards, teachers, and reformers; may they exercise right judgments and fair treatments. Give them faith, both in the abilities of your errant children to change and in their own abilities to help make these changes happen. May you grant them an extra measure of love and patience for which you will eternally bless them a hundredfold. Amen.

SAINT CYPRIAN OF CARTHAGE, C. 200–258

Born in North Africa of pagan parents, Cyprian became a Christian in 246 and was chosen bishop of Carthage in 248. When Carthage suffered a severe epidemic of the plague, its inhabitants blamed Christians for its spread. A persecution ensued, and Cyprian was arrested, tried, and beheaded on September 14, 258.

▶ In His Image and Likeness

Jesus, Teacher of all people, remember your children. Grant us, your children and followers, that we may attain your image and likeness. May we find that you are a just Judge and a good God who is not severe. Amen.

SAINT CLEMENT OF ALEXANDRIA, C. 150–C. 215

A theologian, philosopher, and Father of the early Church, Clement was probably born in Greece, but he was educated at the catechetical school in Alexandria, which he later headed.

▶ Rising From Sleep

To you, O Master, who loves all people, I hasten on rising from sleep; by your mercy I go forth to do your work, and I pray to you: help me at all times, in everything; deliver me from every evil thing of this world and from every attack of the devil; save me and bring me to your Eternal Kingdom. For you are my Creator, the Giver and Provider of everything good; in you is all my hope, and to you I ascribe glory, now and ever, and to the ages of ages.

MACARIUS OF EGYPT, 300–390

Born in Egypt, Macarius withdrew to the desert at the age of thirty, where he sternly disciplined his body by vigils, fasting, and other penances. He was given a wealth of spiritual gifts, including healing, discernment, prophecy, and exorcism. He lived to the age of ninety.

▶ Prayer to Charles de Foucauld, 1858–1916

Charles, you heard a call from God to live with those who had been rejected and marginalized. We are thankful for your heroic witness, and we ask your intercession now, on behalf of all who are poor and those who, in evangelical witness, live in solidarity with, and among them, as visible signs of the ministry of reconciliation which God has committed to us through Jesus Christ. May all come to understand and live the solidarity which you modeled with your life and death. Amen.

A French soldier stationed in Algeria, Charles left the Army to explore Morocco. At St. Augustine Church in Paris, Charles was miraculously "converted" to a life of prayer and service. He was ordained a priest and set up residence on the Morocco-Algeria frontier "to work among the lambs who were most neglected." He was assassinated by members of the Sensi sect from Libya.

▶ Prayer to Saint Martin de Porres, 1579–1639

We lift our hearts in serene confidence and devotion to you, dear Saint Martin. Aware of your unbridled and helpful charity to all levels of society, as well as your own humility, we ask your help. Pour out upon our families the precious gift of your generous and loving care; show people of all races and colors the paths of justice and unity. Implore our Father in heaven for the coming of his kingdom, so that, through mutual benevolence in God, men and women may increase the fruits of grace, and the merits and rewards of eternal life. Amen.

A Dominican brother, Martin de Pores was born in Lima, Peru, the son of a Spanish nobleman and a young freed Black slave. His life of devotion and service took the form of caring for the sick, establishing an orphanage and hospital for the poor children of the slums, and even setting up a shelter for stray dogs and cats.

▶ Prayer to Saint Monica, c. 331–387

Exemplary Mother of Saint Augustine, you tenaciously pursued your wayward son, not with wild threats, but with endless prayers to God. We ask that you intercede for all mothers so that they may draw their own children to God as you did. Show them the way to remain close to their children, even those who have strayed from the nest and the right paths in life. Amen.

Born in Carthage, Monica was the mother of Saint Augustine. When she was widowed about 371, Monica renounced all worldly pleasures and ministered to the poor and orphaned while still working toward the conversion of her wayward son Augustine. Monica followed Augustine to Milan where she became a disciple of Saint Ambrose, and she used every possible strategy to bring Augustine in contact with this holy man. Finally Augustine converted. God had finally granted Monica's wish to see her son baptized. She died at the age of fifty-six.

▶ Prayer Asking for the Intercession of Saint Monica and Saint Augustine

O Father, you are the comfort of those who are afflicted and the salvation of those who hope in you. With mercy, you accepted the tears of our beloved Saint Monica for the conversion of her errant son, Augustine. Grant that, through the powerful intercession of these two saints, we may weep over our own sins and receive your forgiveness. We ask this in the name of your Son, Jesus Christ Our Lord. Amen.

▶ Prayer to Saints Perpetua and Felicity

Dear Perpetual and Felicity, watch over all mothers and children who are separated from each other because of war or persecution. Show a special care for mothers who are imprisoned. Guide them to follow your example of faith and courage. Amen.

Two African mothers from Carthage in North Africa, Perpetua was a young married woman with a nursing child at her breast; Felicity was a slave and eight months pregnant. Both were thrown to the wild animals in the amphitheater.

Bibliography and Acknowledgments

||||||||

Agunwa, C., *More Than Once*. London: Longman, 1967: "Avert This Evil."

Augustine, Saint, *The Confessions*. London: Burns, Oates, and Washbourne, 1923: "For Mercy," "Prayer for the Sick."

Brown, J. T., *Among the Bantu Nomads*. London: Seeley, Service & Co., 1926: "For Rain."

Buhlmann, W., *The Chosen Peoples*. Slough, England: St. Paul, 1982: "For Protection When Misfortune Strikes."

Dieterlen, G., ed., *Textes sacrés d'Afrique Noire*. Paris: Gallimard, 1965: "Bless My Hand, My Creator," "Let Peace Reign," "For Safety From Evil," "May We Have No Accidents," "For Help During a Difficult Birth," "Surround Your Children With Your Power, Lord," "For Help During a Difficult Birth," "May We Have No Accidents," "Strengthen Me and My Children," "For the Health of My Child," "For Strength in My Life, "So That I Return Safe and Sound," "Returning From a Journey," "Save Me From Ruin." Used by permission.

di Nola, A. M., *The Prayers of Man*. London: Heinemann, 1962: "To Be Safe," "For Fruitfulness," "To Make Good Use of the Power Granted Us," "God Has Turned Away," "Litany," "To Make the Father Known," "I Offer My Child to You, Lord," "We Are Your Sons," "I Turn to You, Father," "Our Lord, Our Moon," "I Turn to God in Prayer." Used by permission.

Donovan, V., *Christianity Rediscovered*. SCM, 1978: "Credo."

Du Bois, W. E. B., *Prayers for Dark People*. Amherst: University of Massachusetts Press, 1980: "Lift Our Hearts."

Evans-Pritchard, E., *Nuer Religion*. Oxford: Clarendon Press, 1956: "Remove Us From Evil," "Let the Wound Heal."

Finnegan, R., *Oral Literature in Africa*. London: Clarendon Press, 1970: "For a Peaceful Death for My Mother."

Finnegan, R., ed., *The Penguin Book of Oral Poetry*. London: Allen Lane, 1978: "You Loved Me Before Creation," "Select Wisdom," "Give Rain to Your People," "Blessing of a Child," "Let God Shield You."

Gaba, Christian R., *Scriptures of an African People*. New York: NOK Publishers, 1973: "For Prosperity," "For Prosperity, Health, Children, and Long Life," "To Always Be in Good Health." Used by permission.

Guilleband, R., "The Idea of God in Ruandi-Urandi," in *African Ideas of God*, London: Edinburgh House Press, 1950: "If Only You Could Help Me."

Harris, W. T., "The Idea of God Among the Mende," in *African Ideas of God*: London: Edinburgh House Press, 1950, "For Good Fortune," "For My Son."

Hollis, A. C., *The Nandi-Their Language and Folklore*. Oxford: Clarendon Press, 1909: "Keep Watch Over Us."

Hughes, Langston, ed., *Poems From Black Africa*. Bloomington: Indiana University Press, 1963: "The Nativity."

Idowu, E. B., *Olodumare: God in Yoruba Belief*. London: Longman, 1962: "Look After Our Children," "A Peaceful Death," "To Treat Matters With Careful Consideration."

Kenyatta, J., *Facing Mount Kenya*. London: Secker & Warburg, 1961: "Guide My Steps in Peace," "Guard This Homestead."

Kenyatta, J., *My People of Kikuyu*. London: Oxford, 1966: "God, Our Great Elder."

Konadu, A., *A Woman in Her Prime*. London: Heinemann, 1967: "For Remedies."

Lindblom, G., *The Akamba in British East Africa*. Uppsala: K. W. Appelbergs, 1916: "In Thanksgiving for the Birth of a Child."

Mbiti, John, *The Prayers of African Religion*. London: SPCK, 1975: "Bless Me," "For Rain," "God, the Word," "For Abundance and Health," "The Lord Gives Life," "May God Bless You," "For Goodness to Remain," "For Plentiful Blessings," "Help My Sick Child," "God, Continue Your Help," "God, You Are the Source of Life," "Give Us Health," "Help Us Through This Sickness." Used by permission.

Moreau, J., "Les Pygmées" in *Parole et mission*, XI, 1960: "In Thanksgiving for a Large Family."

Nyom, B., "Le sacré et l'unité de l'hommé," Doctoral Thesis, Lille, 1964: "God Take Your Portion."

Paton, Alan. *Instrument of Thy Peace.* New York: The Seabury Press, 1968: "Instrument of Peace,"

Pawelzik, Fritz, ed., *I Lie on My Mat and Pray.* New York: Friendship Press, 1964: "We Drink In the Beauty of Your Creation," "God Glistens on the Grasses," "Bless This," "Feed Our Hungry Brothers and Sisters," "My Only Help in Misery," "For a Job," "The Chief's Prayer," "For the Future Leaders of Our Land," "Our Country Needs Us," "I Am Not Afraid." Used by permission.

Pawelzik, Fritz, ed., *I Sing Your Praises All Day Long.* New York: Friendship Press, 1967: "Lord, We Give Thanks for Everything," "A Fisherman's Prayer," "For Honesty in Business," "For an Understanding of God and an End to Fear," "For God's Grace." Used by permission.

Poirier, R., Personal collection, Bethel Park, Pennsylvana 15102, n.d.: "God, Provider of Life," "Credo Two," "So We No Longer Have Doubts," "The Fire Blessing," "Father, Bless This Fire," "Father, Thank You."

Roscoe, J., *The Baktiara or Banyoro.* Cambridge: The University Press, 1923: "For Success."

Samburu Manuscript Prayers, Consolata Fathers, London, n.d.: "For a Peaceful Life," "For Everlasting Life," "God, Protect Our Elders," "Dawn of My God," "God, Be Our Safeguard," "For Food," "God, Be Our Children's Guardian," "May God Be Good," "For a Sweet and Everlasting Life," "May God Be With You," "To Always Rise Higher," "To Heal a Mother," "God Grant Me Children," "Guard Us From Danger," "I Want to Be Close to You, God," "Sacrificial Prayer for Eternal Life," "Prayer for an Assembly of the Elders," "God, Be by My Side," "Do Not Reject Us," "God, Take Care of My Needs," "God, Make Me Walk in Peace," "May God Grant What You Desire," "Guard Our Group," "Before a Journey," "Before a Meeting," "For a Bride," "May God Enlarge Everything That Is Yours," "May God Watch Over You," "Forgive Our Unintentional Sins," "Grant Us Prosperity," "For a Long and Fruitful Life," "God, Be My Relief," "To Walk Along a Good Road," "Watch Over Us While We Sleep," "Be Our Support."

Senghor, Léopold Sédar. *Prose and Poetry.* London: Oxford University Press, 1965: "Prayer for Peace and Brotherhood."

Shorter, Aylward, "Divine Call and Human Response," in *The Way,* vol. 23, no. 39: "For a Peaceful Night."

Shorter, Aylward, ed., *Prayer in the Religious Traditions of Africa*. Oxford, 1975: "Give Us Your Blessing," "Accept the Morning Greeting," "Success for Our Crops," "O God, Lead My Steps," "Give Us Rain, "Bless Us and All We Have," "Keep Me Safe From Sickness," "To Remove Suffering," "Let Us Walk in Health," "May We Not Die Young," "For a Quick Recovery," "Help Me Sleep Well." Used by permission.

Smith, Edwin W., ed, *African Ideas of God*. London: Edinburgh House Press, 1950: "God, Our Great Spirit," "God, Creator of All Life," "I Am Hungry, Feed Me," "Hush, Child," "Prayer to the Father of Our Fathers," "O Great Spirit."

Sundkler, B., *Bantu Prophets in South Africa*. London: Oxford, 1948: "Our King."

Tescaroli, Cirillo, "Catholic Elite," October, 1981: "To Walk Straight On the Path," "May We Sleep in Peace."

Tutschek, C. A., *Grammar of the Galla (Boran) Language*. Munich, 1845: "For Danger to Pass By."

Tutu, Desmond, *An African Prayer Book*. London: Hodder & Stoughton, 1985: "In Victory."

Westermann, D., *The Shilluk People*. Berlin: Dietrich Reimer, 1912: "A Night Prayer."

Williams, J. T., *Africa's God*. Boston College Graduate School, 10 vols., 1936-7: "Sorrow."

Wilson, M., *Communal Rituals of the Nyakyusa*. London: Oxford University Press, 1959: "For an End to Theft," "Prayer of General Confession." Used by permission.

First Line Index

||||||||

A child is like a rare bird 56
After the crucifixion of my country for over 400 years 103
Ah God, you know this is my son 77
All our forebears, come and eat kola 38
As for me, God has devoured me 91

Bless this tree; make it grow... 43
Brightness, help this man that he may be well 90
Buyers and sellers 31

Charles, you heard a call from God to live with those who... 112
Come, Lord, and cover me with the night 96
Creator God, we announce your goodness ... 1
Creator Lord, through whom everything on this earth grows 24

Dear Perpetual and Felicity, watch over all... 114
Do not reject us, O God 67

Exemplary Mother of Saint Augustine... 113

Father, thank you for your revelation 93
Father, you are the origin of all that is holy... 101
Father, you called me to give up all... 108
For your blessing we thank you, God: faith in you 27
Friend, God, who is in this village 74

God, accept the morning greeting 11
God agrees: let us pray to God 45
God, agree with us; wake up 90

About the Author

||||||||||

Anthony Gittins, CSSp, was trained as an anthropologist and worked as a missionary in West Africa for eight years. Currently, Father Gittins is the Bishop F. X. Ford Professor of Missiology at Catholic Theological Union in Chicago and also serves as a retreat director and speaker before national and international audiences. He has done anthropological/theological research and teaching in Pakistan, the Philippines, Australia, the Trobriand Islands, and Kiribati, a chain of islands in the Central Pacific Ocean. Father Gittins also works with homeless people in Chicago.